DF

ALLEN RIDER GUIDES

RIDING: THE GAME OF POLO

ALLEN RIDER GUIDES

Riding: The Game of Polo

Richard Hobson

J.A. Allen
London

Published in Great Britain by
J.A. ALLEN & Co. Ltd
1 Lower Grosvenor Place
London
SW1W OEL

British Library Cataloguing in Publication Data
A catalogue record for this book is available from the British Library.

ISBN 0-85131-581-X

Text illustrations: Maggie Raynor
Text and cover design: Nancy Lawrence

Typeset by Textype Typesetters, Cambridge
Printed by Huntsman 'Offset', Singapore

Frontispiece: Riding off. The rider in the foreground is slightly twisted in the saddle to offset the coming 'bump', and hence his leg is misplaced from its normal position.

Contents

Foreword
by Lieut. Col. A.F. Harper, DSO

This is an update of the excellent booklet written twenty years ago by Dick Hobson (a high-goal player and expert horseman).

The legendary Tommy Hitchcock is said to have defined the best player as 'the one who hits the ball the furthest and the oftenest'. 'Furthest' is easy to understand, but what about 'oftenest'?

At any given moment the player must know where the ball is and where the goals, side-lines and all the other players are. Then he must think who is going to hit it next, where to, who will get there first, can I get it, or should I take a man out, where shall I go? The man who gets the right answer 'oftenest', always turns out to be the man who hits the ball 'oftenest'.

All this high-speed thinking means that a player must ride without thinking – and yet no two horses are quite alike, so he must remember which one he is riding.

In the background is the training, buying, selling and feeding of horses which a player must know something about, the more the better for him.

All this makes polo the most fascinating game in the world, and you will also make a variety of friends whose only thing in common may be their enthusiasm for the game.

A beginner will find essential help – and an experienced player will find useful reminders – in this book which covers every aspect of the game in a short and clear way.

ALEX HARPER
April, 1993

Introduction

It is assumed that most people about to read this book will have at least watched a polo match and therefore have some inkling as to what the game is about before they start to play it.

The official rules, as published by the Hurlingham Polo Association, can be found at the back of the book and are essential reading for anyone wishing to be involved in the game. Nevertheless it might be helpful to describe in a nutshell how the game of polo is played.

A polo ground measures a maximum of 300 yards in length by 200 yards in width, and has a goal mouth at either end denoted by two goalposts.The game is played by two teams, each of four players, mounted on ponies of any height. The aim is to score more goals than your opponents. Each player is handicapped from -2 to +10. No player may play with his left hand.

The polo ball, which is a small (up to 3.5 ins diameter) ball made of willow or bamboo root, is hit with a polo stick made of cane and measuring 48-54 ins long with a cylindrical wooden head set at a angle to the shaft.

The duration of play is divided into periods (or chukkas) of seven minutes each, with three-minute intervals between the periods and a five-minute interval at half-time. The game may be of three, four, five or six chukkas. Players use the intervals to change ponies.

Play is supervised by two mounted umpires and an off-the-field referee. It is the umpires' task to interpret the rules to the best of their ability and to try to ensure fair play. They are empowered to award penalties (free goals and free hits) and to disqualify players or ponies for any rule infringements.

Each time a goal is scored the players change ends, the eventual winners being the side that has scored the most goals.

Development of the Game

One can learn a great deal from history - providing the right lessons are derived. It may therefore be helpful briefly to recount the origins and progress of the game.

Polo appears to have been played in Persia around 600 BC. A sort of polo was first observed by Englishmen being played by frontier tribes in India and was imported into England by the 10th Hussars, who played their first ever match in England on Hounslow Heath against the 9th Lancers in 1871. There were eight players on each side and they rode very small ponies. In a very short time, it became 'a soldier's game', for the very good reasons that the game produced and demanded high standards of horsemanship and **horsemastership**; it required fitness, discipline, quick reactions and a degree of courage; and furthermore, the game itself was fun, took a short time to complete and did not interfere unduly with an officer's duties. In short it was an excellent medium for the training of officers.

But, of course, those were the days when not only the Cavalry, but also the Gunners and even Infantry had horses on their establishments and all officers had to go through elementary Riding School at Sandhurst and Woolwich. The development of the game was therefore centred on the army. In 1914, before World War I was declared, England had beaten America with a team comprised of Cavalry officers. Even in 1910 a scratch Army team visited California and swept the board, to such an extent that in the final match, the opposing players refused to turn up and surrendered the cups without contest.

But alas, the holocaust of 1914-1918 cost Britain its best players and ponies, and it wasn't until 1922 that the Argentines sent a most respected team to England, lead by that doyen of polo players, Lewis Lacey, a fine horseman. This team had lovely ponies and were respected and admired. So in between the Wars, polo revived. In 1919, the height limit for ponies (previously 14.2 hh) was abolished. In the late 1920s and early 1930s, teams came from

India to play in England, the best being Jaipur, who were unbeaten that particular summer. Perhaps the best game of polo ever witnessed was at Rugby, when Jaipur, a superb team, consisting of Jaipur, Hanut, Abbey and Prithi were opposed by Lt Col Vivian Lockett, Capt 'Chicken' Walford (both 17/21 L) and Capts Peter Dollar (4H) and Friz Fowler (RHA). At the beginning of the last chukka, the Army team was leading Jaipur by one goal. In the chukka interval there was a great carfuffle in the Jaipur pony lines and it transpired that they had pulled out their best ponies for that last chukka, during which they scored three goals to the Army's nil. That was a supreme example of 'pony power'.

It was about this time, too, that a professional element appeared in polo, headed by such as the Baldings and Johnny Traill from Argentina. They always had ponies to sell!

The conclusions to be learned from all this is that horsemanship and horsemastership are of paramount importance in polo. Army officers had the advantage of being taught to ride and were endlessly in the saddle. With the demise of horsed cavalry, however, the predominance of Army influence on polo rapidly decreased. It has now become more professional and only those with money can afford the enormous cost of buying ponies and of playing the game. In particular, Argentinian and other players and ponies are imported for the season, and their philosophy in the schooling of ponies and of play now predominates. Alas!

The Changing Face of Polo

To be specific about the differences today, these can be summarised as follows:

- In the high-handicap tournaments, the teams are usually composed of the 'patron', a rich man who imports from abroad (mostly from Argentina and the Americas) high handicap-rated players, together with a flood of ponies.
- Of course the 'patrons' wish to play, but being of low handicap they cannot realistically fit in with the high-goal 'professionals'. Hence the 'pros' hog the ball and endeavour to win the match by their own efforts. Thus the team game goes by the board, and this is causing a deterioration of standards.
- The ponies (and the 'pros') cost fabulous sums of money. In the

past, £500 was an absolutely top price for a perfectly trained animal. Nowadays a good pony can cost £20,000 or more.

• As opposed to pre- and post-World War II, there are all too few English trainers of polo ponies. Foreign-trained ponies are mass-produced (there is an endless supply in the Argentine) and their methods of breaking do not ensure that their animals are balanced, supple and obedient to the leg, with free forward movement, before specialist training for polo is attempted. In the 1950s and 60s it was rare, and most unusual, for an Argentinian pony to be given a prize at the Polo Pony Show. Which is not to say that the Argentine pony is no good: many beautiful animals are imported, but they need reschooling before they achieve the training required for a top-class pony.

1

General Principles and Players' Duties

It has already been indicated that the game of polo is a game for horsemen. To be a successful player, complete control of the pony at full gallop is necessary. Futhermore, the game itself requires a high standard of discipline and unselfish team play. In the past, a good polo team was always 'drilled', i.e. each member knew exactly what to do in any given circumstance and his reactions had to be instantaneous. Good players must know where to go – and quickly – during the game; what can and cannot be done during play; what penalties are involved in certain instances; where in principle the ball should be hit.

At its best, polo is a game of quick thinking, played by fit young men, who are good horsemen and who – on the polo ground – do as they are expected to do or are told to do. Played well, it is probably the fastest game in the world. There are two elements in it – the player and the pony. They are complementary and indivisible.

But these considerations need not inhibit an unambitious player in older age, who knows the game, enjoys himself, gets good exercise and, hopefully, at the same time, is instructing the young beginner. Indeed, such players are the backbone of the game.

General Principles of the Game

- Polo is a **team game**. The object of the game is to **score goals**, and this can best be done by **passing the ball to each other**.

■ Apart from hitting the ball, each player has his job to do, all the time, in **neutralising his opposite number**. If you 'take your man' you will playing for your team.

■ The most important participant in the game is your **pony**. The better it is schooled, and the better you ride it, the more you will enjoy the game. In fact, the more you school and the more you practise, the better you will be. If you do neither, no one will want you on his side.

■ Keep your position and ride your man. A shot prevented is a shot made. 'Ball hunting' denotes a selfish player and the team and the results of the game will suffer.

■ Napoleon said: 'Le galop, le galop et toujours le galop.' This applies also to polo; great exertion is needed.

■ The only words needed in a game, apart from captain's instructions, are: '**Ball**'; '**Leave it**'; '**Man**' and such other team cries as '**Centre**'; '**Here**' as may be arranged. **Never** shout '**Right**'; '**Go on**'; or '**Ride him**'. **Always** do what you are told from behind, no matter who tells you (except an opponent!).

■ One of the worst shots at polo is to hit across your opponent's back line without scoring. It means the intiative immediately passes to him. To do so, if making a shot from a difficult angle, is inexcusable. Therefore, when in doubt, hit the ball into the centre; or if some way out and a goal is not certain, do an approach shot before shooting for goal.

■ When galloping down the ground, the way to find out which man you should be marking is to count 'heads in front'. If there is an odd number, and one more of your opponents to your side, your man is in front of you and you must push on to catch him. If an even number, and two of each side, then you are spare. In this case, **if defending** you must **hold back** and take the next man. If attacking, however, don't look for an opponent to mark you! If there are two of your own side to one of theirs in front of you in defence, let one man go past you and take the next man.

So, in defence, take the right man; but in attack, try to remain free. But remember, the game turns very quickly and you must always be ready to get your man in defence.

■ Close with your man at once, and try to get your knee in front of his. If you can do this you stand more chance of 'controlling' him and of hitting the ball if it comes to you.

■ Hit to the side of the ground when defending in your own half. Always hit to the centre of your opponent's half of the ground, however.

■ When attacking and it is clear that the opposing Back, or No. 3, is going to do a backhander, the attacking No. 3 and Back should not follow one behind the other, but divide up the ground between them so as to try and anticipate and meet the backhander and so continue the attack.

■ On the other hand, always 'turn up' to take on one of your own side's backhanders.

■ When the ball goes out, or behind, or when a penalty is awarded, **gallop** to your position. Hanging about slows up the game, and if you are not in your place early, you will not be ready to adjust your position, nor to receive your captain's orders, whereby you may be able to save or score a goal when the ball is in play again.

■ Play the game for your side; and always remember that however aggravated you may be by other players, or your pony, or the umpire, it is, after all, only a game.

■ Polo is a game of quick thinking and quick action; of anticipation and rapid decisions; of some danger and therefore high tensions. Learn to play with your head up, looking about you so as to be aware what the other players are doing. This will help you to remain mentally and physically relaxed. You need only keep your eyes fixed on the ball, just prior to the moment of striking.

■ Never 'hang about'. Half a length on a turn may make all the difference to the result of the game. Many are called, but few are chosen to a handicap of 3 or higher. But all can enjoy it if it is played in the proper spirit.

Duties of the Players

NO. 1

- Like Uriah the Hittite, he must always be in the forefront of the battle in attack, and be persistently **offensive**.
- In defence, he must stick to the opposing back like a limpet, and by all (fair) means prevent him hitting the ball.
- By lying just offside, he should make the Back take the initiative from him; but not so far off side that he cannot get to the Back in defence.
- He should make himself an accurate shot at goal, particularly from close to.
- In general, he should 'work' the centre of the ground except when riding Back off the ground, to give a clear run for somebody else. Nos. 2 and 3 'work' the sides of the ground.
- If in doubt, he should always turn towards the centre, and be 'optimistic' about turning up.
- He should always gallop for the forlorn hope.
- Even if getting the worst of a ride-off, he must persevere and hustle the opponent.

NO. 2

- He is the 'second forward', and his prime duty is to 'make' goals. He also must be mentally attuned to **attack**.
- He must be ready to take the place of No. 1 if necessary.
- He must pass the ball so that his No. 1 can get it and **not** the opposing Back.
- He should only have a shot at goal when it is a nigh certainty.
- He must never allow the opposing No. 3 (often the best player in the opposing side) to ride loose.
- He must remember that the goal scoring, and hence the match-winning potential of his side, largely depends on him.

NO. 3

- He is the pivot of the side and the link between forwards and back. By his positional play, No. 3 must hold his side together, and he should be **defensive** minded.
- He should feed his forwards by accurately passing the ball to them. He should not turn on the ball, which slows up the game,

but hit long backhanders.

- In defence, he should never let Back have to compete with two men.
- When Back goes forward, he must interchange and stay back.
- If, when attacking, the ball goes behind him, he must invariably turn back.
- If he finds himself in No. 1 or No. 2's place, he should stay there until a favourable opportunity occurs for regaining his position.
- He should be the best mounted man on the side, as well as the best hitter. He has got to do more galloping and turning than anyone else, and must never miss an opportunity of supporting his forwards in an attack.
- He should hit his backhanders at an angle, so as to avoid the legs of oncoming ponies and so that his No. 2 can pick up his pass.

BACK

- It is his prime duty to prevent the other side from scoring goals. His steadiness should be as proverbial as the Rock of Gibraltar.
- When in doubt, he should turn back. Defence must always be his predominant instinct.
- He must avoid being 'slipped' by the opposing No. 1.
- Only when covered by another member of his side should he meet the ball.
- Nevertheless, he should be on the alert for an opportunity to 'go through'. But he should not go through unless he can go right through and stands a chance of having a shot at goal.
- He should never be far from the centre of the ground, and must learn to *anticipate* where the ball is likely to go.
- First and foremost, he must play a safe game, keep the 'back door' shut and be certain of hitting his backhanders, so as to give freedom and confidence to the rest of his side to attack.

2

Positional Diagrams

The 'drills' referred to in Chapter 1 are required in order to initiate from the start (or restart) the best forms of attack or defence.

Study, for instance, Fig. 1. The aim at the start of both Nos. 1 should be to meet the throw-in and take the ball down the ground and score. It has often been done. However, the opposing Back and No. 3 must be so placed that they can defend. Alternatively, if the ball comes through the line-up, No. 3 or Back should hit the ball so that their No. 1 can pick it up and score. In any case, Nos 1 and 2 must go up and defence must be left to No. 3 and Back. If, on the other hand, the opposing No. 1 does pick up the ball at the throw-in, then the defending No. 1 must go with him and do his best to prevent him from scoring. In this case the No. 2 must still go up, replace No.1 in defence and mark the opposing Back.

Once the game has started, the rest of the scenario falls into place, and the remaining positional diagrams are a matter for team preference. Some like one way; others another. In Figs 2–5 it largely depends on which player is hitting and on his power and accuracy.

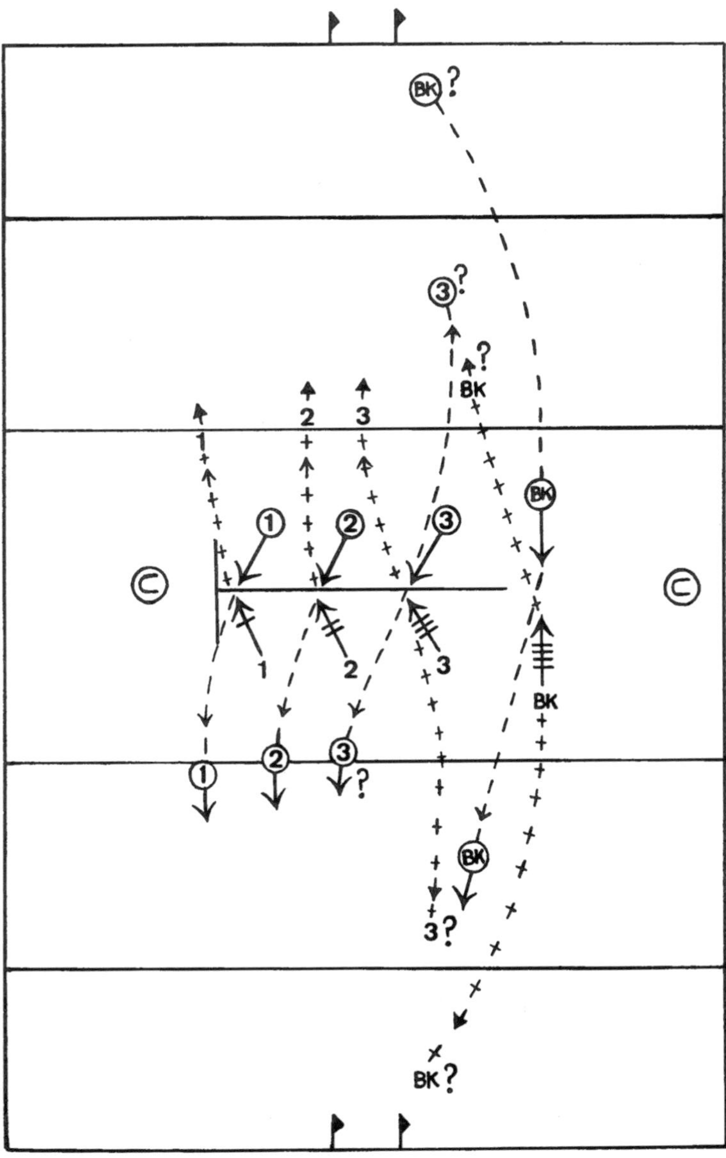

Fig. 1 The throw-in.

U = umpire

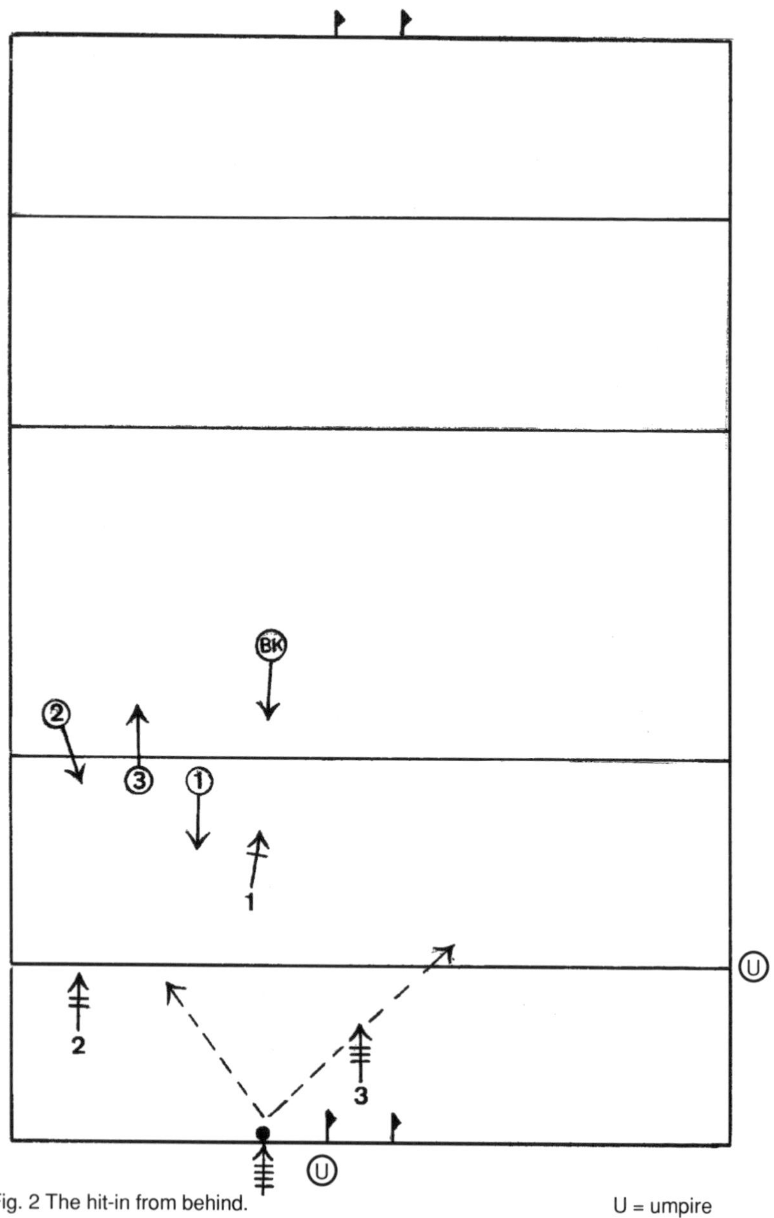

Fig. 2 The hit-in from behind.

U = umpire

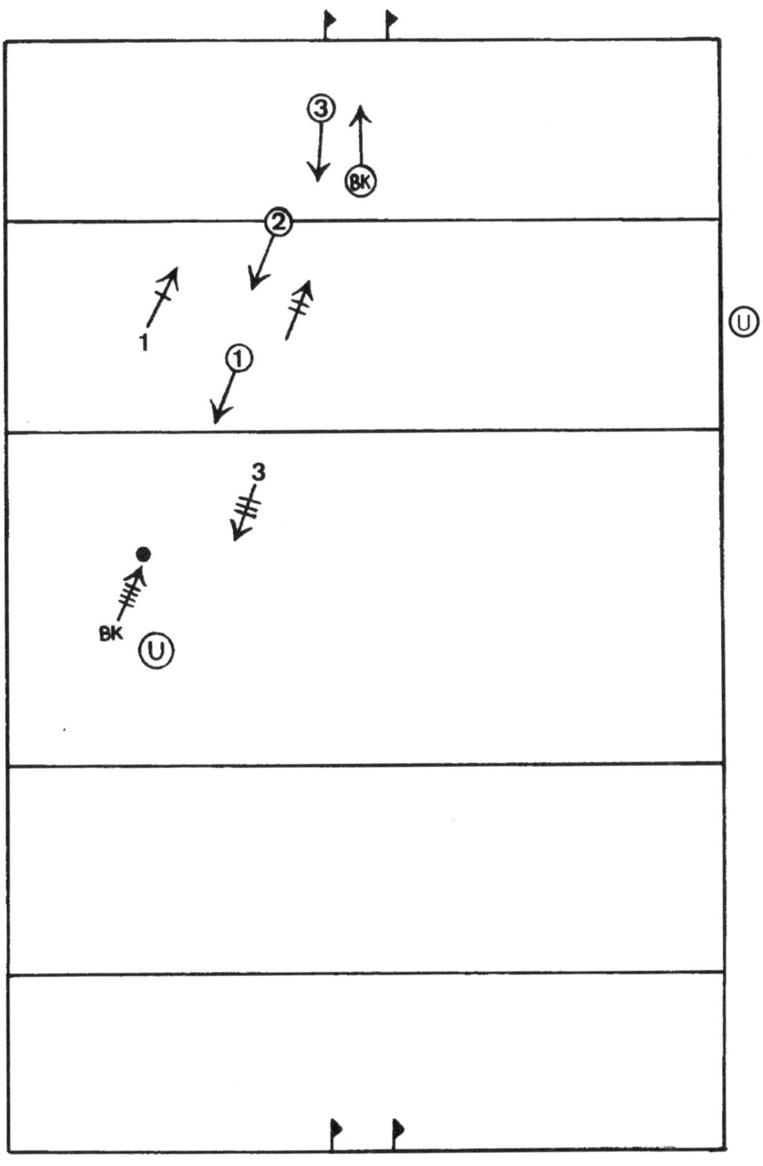

Fig. 3 The free-hit.

U = umpire

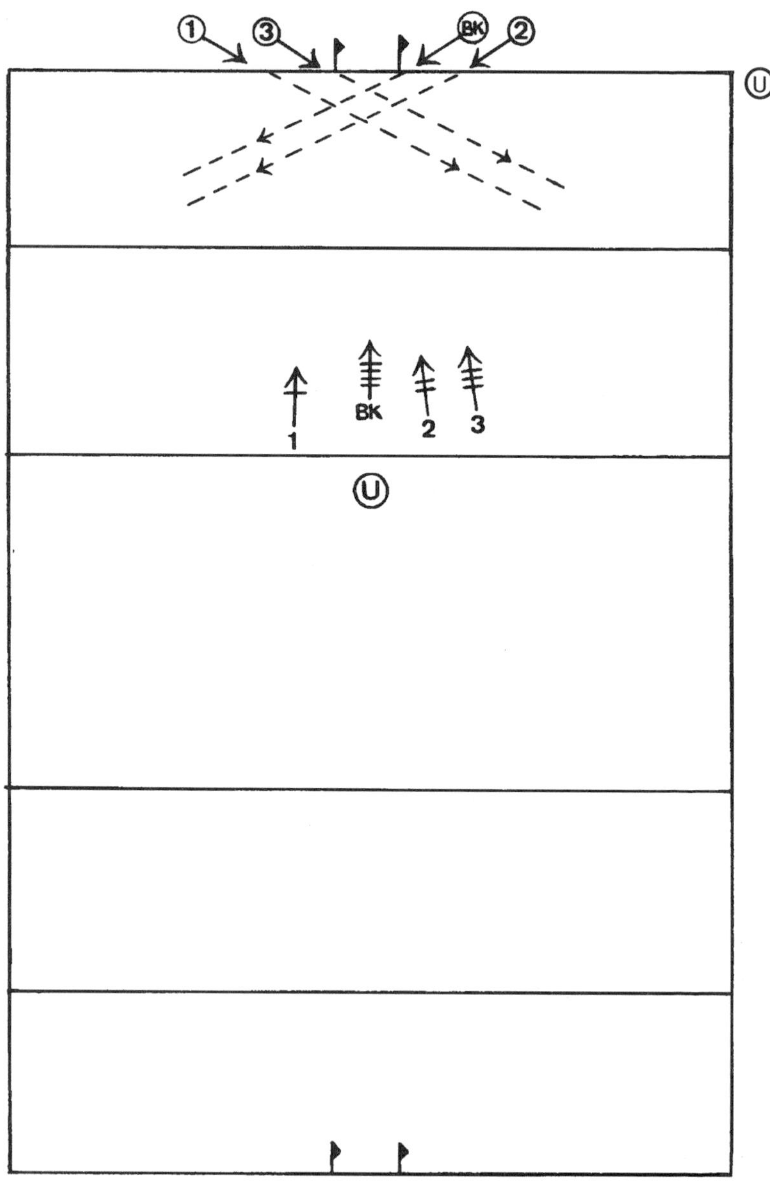

Fig. 4 The 30-yard or 40-yard free hit. U = umpire

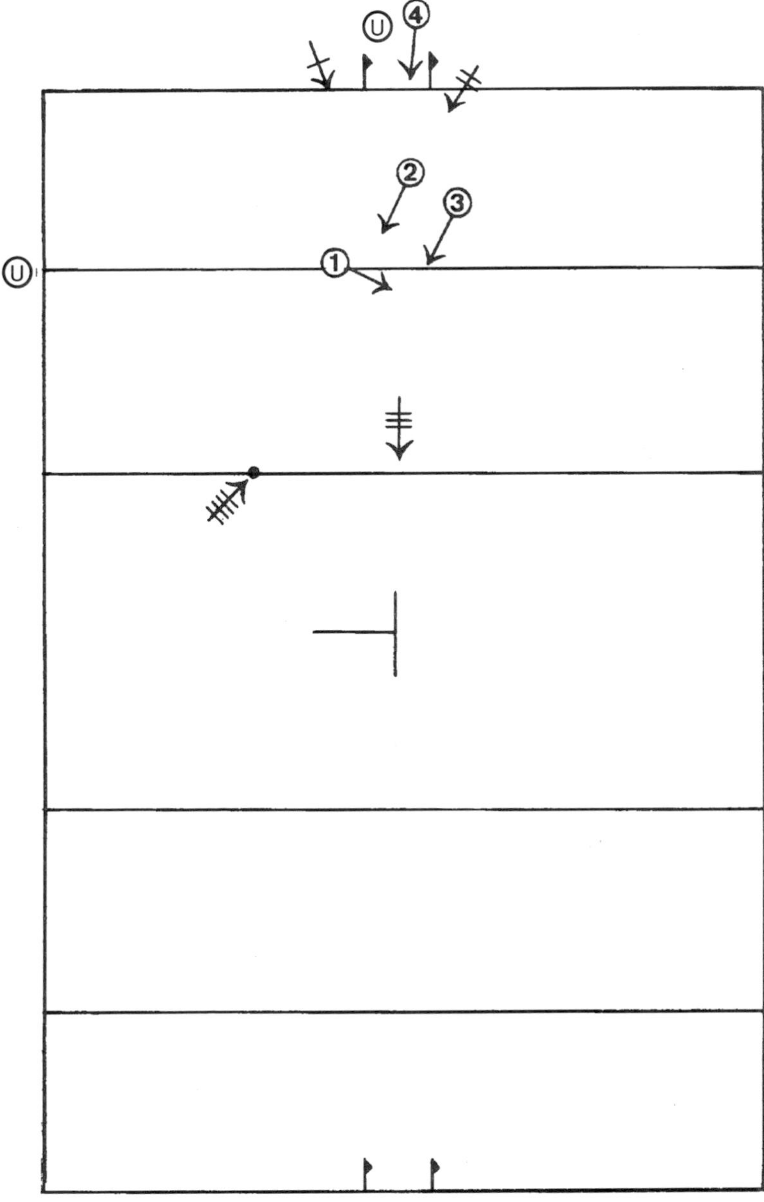

Fig. 5 The 60-yard hit.

U = umpire

Fig. 6 Action at throw-in. White attacking to right, black to left.

- Black No. 1, with his stick correcty on his nearside, has pushed past his opposite number, having failed to intercept the throw-in, and goes up.
- The ball has gone through the line-up, but black No. 2 still goes up
- White No. 3 seems to have the ball and black No. 3 turns to go back (hopefully to hit a backhander to his forwards).
- White No. 2 has incorrectly turned back and there is no one for white No. 3 to hit to, white No. 1 having been temporarily impeded.

3
Ponies

It must be clear from the foregoing that the handiness, suppleness, speed, courage and quick reactions of a player's mount are of paramount importance. It takes but half a length on a turn to get the best of an opponent and to have an unhindered shot at the ball. Depending on the class of polo to be played, so depends the type of pony required.

The Beginner's Pony

Primarily this must be 'easy' – not necessarily very fast, but handy, and not too tall so that it is easy to hit the ball off. Polo is a complicated game and it takes *time* to learn it. The beginner will have no fun and will not learn the game if he has to spend his time wrestling with his pony. Nor is it likely that having to go very fast he will hit the ball at all. A smallish 'stuffy' type of pony, which doesn't take too much out of itself and is not too highly bred is, moreover, likely to stand up to more work and not suffer from 'knocking the ball about' in practice, as well as playing in formal chukkas. Many ponies of this sort are imported from the Argentine each year.

Ponies for More Experienced Players

After overcoming the beginner's stages of playing the game, supplemented hopefully by long periods of 'knocking about' and schooling, the young player should begin to know what sort of pony he wants, and above all, what sort of pony he can ride. Very high-class ponies are high mettled, require an experienced horseman and are nowadays excessively expensive. In any case riders have their own 'handwriting'. Some will like one thing, another something else; 'one man's meat is another man's poison'; or, like Mr Jorrocks said:' 'oo shall counsel a man in the choice of a wife or an 'oss?'

There are, of course, two ways of mounting yourself. The first, the cheapest and by far the most satisfactory, is to 'make' your own ponies. This requires *time* (primarily), expertise, patience, horsemanship and horsemastership as well as knowledge of the game. Regarding the last point, however good a horseman a man is, he cannot bring a pony up to top class unless he plays and knows the game. Riding-school standards must certainly form the *basis* of any schooling. But the schooling for polo can most conveniently be done, not necessarily by a high-goal player, but at least by a 'polo horseman'.

There are many examples of such. Undoubtedly the best was the late Harold Freeborn, who was Master of Horse to Lord Cowdray for many years. A superb and most sympathetic horseman, he probably produced more good ponies than anyone else. Another was Harold Thomason, Master of Horse to Lord Dalmeny (as he then was) and then to Sir Harold Wernher. A beautiful horseman, he learned his equitation among the cowboys in California and knew what 'balance' and 'handiness' meant.

I repeat, 'polo depends on ponies' – at whatever level you wish to play. Very fast high-class animals are not required for club games, where enjoyment, exercise and a challenge are all that is sought. Indeed, really the basis of the game is enjoyment. That depends, however, on one's ponies; if they go well – whatever the standard or importance of the game – then you will have enjoyed yourself. The reverse is also true. Those who are horsemen with an eye for a ball and games sense will eventually aspire to higher things, however, and they will need higher class ponies.

The Top-class Pony

I firmly believe the really top-class pony is born, not 'made'. So what are the properties of this magical animal?

Most of the best are Thoroughbred, and are more intelligent and have more scope than a half-bred (although this is not always the case). The pony must have speed and instant acceleration. It must enjoy the game (which comes from sympathetic training) and do its best to bring you to the ball. It must be bold, determined, and invincible in combat with other ponies. It must respond instantaneously to any indications to the mouth or the rider's balance that are given. Indeed it may well anticipate them. The perfect mouth was once described as like 'pulling through butter' – and the more insistent the pull (but not a rough one) the quicker the pony will respond.

These sort of animals are rare indeed. They will have been initially schooled by a sympathetic polo horseman. They will rarely be ridden in gag snaffles and a mass of leatherwork to control their head carriage. They will flex their jaws when pressure is applied on their bits and stop by bending their backs, *drawing* up with rounded loins rather than bouncing up with a stiff, hollow back. That makes them much quicker on the turn and so it is easier for the player to control the ball. Which, of course, is all *training*, which takes *time*.

To reinforce this, I invite any man to observe how horses, when free and galloping round a field, stop. It is with their heads down and their backs bent.

Lucky the man who can come to own such a rarity. He can then forget about his pony and concentrate solely on the game, and he and his pony will be as one.

A final word of warning, however. The worst enemy of a polo pony is oats – or whatever heating mixture you give it to eat. Supervision on this is essential, and only the player can be final arbiter. An overfed pony will be over-exuberant and inclined to 'run-on', and damage to the mouth can ensue. Each pony is different. Before the Second World War and playing high-goal polo, the amount of oats given to my ponies varied from 4 lbs to 12 lbs per day. The best of them was on 4lbs!

Polo ponies are not like hunters. They do not leave their stables early in the morning, gallop through mud all day and get home in the dark. They have short, sharp periods of exertion, in (usually) clement weather, and return to their stables quickly. They do not, on the whole, need too much heating food.

Conformation

There is much misconception and misunderstanding about conformation, and it is essential to know what is important and less important concerning the points of a horse.

First, a short digression into anatomy is necessary in order to make clear the natural way a horse performs. All impulsion starts from the loins and the conformation of the spine at this point is important. Those great muscles and nerves which run down the horse's back are attached to the processes on the spine. For complete freedom of movement it is necessary for those processes to be, as it were, open over the loins, to enable the muscles to have free play. Restriction of freedom will come about when the processes are closed, and this occurs when the loins are hollowed or stiff. This is liable to be the result if the horse carries his head too high, or pokes his nose. Lack of impulsion and inability to use itself correctly will follow.

Consider for a moment what a horse does with his head at moments of maximum effort, such as in the act of taking off for a jump, at a full gallop, stopping suddenly when loose in a field, or when recovering from a peck: **he stretches his neck.** This action frees his loins and allows maximum freedom of movement there. If you have any doubts about this, throw your own chin up and your head back and see whether, in this position, you can exert the same strength with your arms and legs as when your head is slightly forward. This factor is absolutely fundamental to all equitation.

No two ponies are precisely the same. Some will have, let us say, the advantage of a particularly good shoulder; another will have perhaps weak hocks, but offset by being very strong over the loins, or even having a roach back, which indicates strength. Strong hocks and a straight hind leg are very important. However, perhaps it would be best to enumerate characteristics which will, in most cases, **debar** an animal's suitability for polo.

- First and foremost must come a wild, ungenerous or 'pig-like' eye. An eye is a difficult thing to judge and even experts can be wrong. It is essential, however, to have a long look at the pony's eye before purchase. Only by correct interpretation of the eye can the character of the animal be ascertained. Calmness, kindness, generosity, courage and a relaxed disposition must be the requirements.

- A badly set on head or a ewe neck will make communication between mouth and loins, as required for polo, impossible.

Fig. 7 *Left*: A well set on head and neck. *Right:* A ewe neck.

- Weak loins, likewise, will inhibit the proper functioning of the 'back end' (quarters and hocks) on which most of the activity of a polo pony depends. Similarly, weak or 'sickle' hocks are a serious disadvantage.

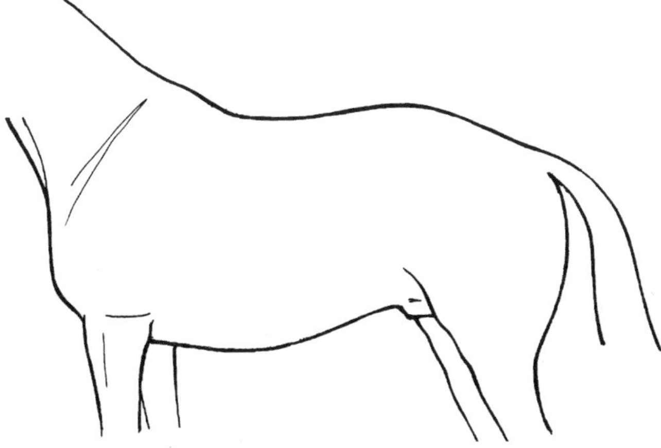

Fig. 8 A slightly roached back.

- Big or flat feet often denote clumsiness – a disadvantage.
- In general, avoid 'overtopped' heavy animals, perhaps with loaded shoulders or too 'thick' in the body. Although probably all right for beginners, they are seldom sufficiently active or supple enough for high-class polo.

There is also one important 'plus' requirement which should be mentioned. When viewed from behind, it is desirable that the animal should be wider through its second thighs than its hips. This gives strength and balance behind the saddle where it is most needed.

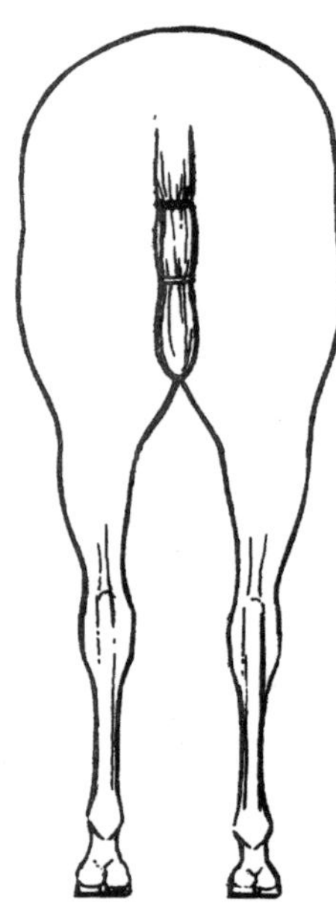

Fig. 9 A proper 'farewell' for a polo pony – wider through the second thighs than through the hips.

4
The Techniques

Riding

This will not be a dissertation on equitation. Many books by eminent authorities have been written on that subject, and the accepted techniques of training the horse apply as a **basic** requirement for the training and riding of polo ponies; but with modifications, **after** the animal has been balanced and persuaded to go forward freely. To progress to further training for polo, the rider should have the conventional firm seat and have suppleness, strength and balance in the saddle. He needs to acquire what is termed an 'independent' seat, meaning that, with the grip of the knees and the constant application of the lower leg in the correct position, the hands and the upper part of the body **above the hips** are free to function as required. More than anything else it is a matter of balance. This ensures that the pony knows where his rider's weight is, and hence can balance itself. A rider who is 'all over the place' in the saddle, with legs, seat, arms and hands flapping, can only confuse his unfortunate mount and the rider's signals will be unclear. Stability and constancy of seat are therefore essential. This requires, above all, **strength**, combined with sensitivity.

To illustrate what is meant it may help to compare the horsemanship of a polo player with that of a dressage expert, who is required to maintain a very upright position with a firm contact on the mouth with movements done at slow paces. The polo player requires his mount to operate mostly on a loose rein, to change legs instantaneously in a flat-out gallop, to stop and turn on the haunches, to change direction and change leg, also at full gallop,

Fig. 10 The sort of equitation that gets polo a bad name. This sketch is based on a photo of a 'high-class player' in 1992. Note:

- Hands behind his pony's ears.
- Sitting back in the saddle
- Knees out, toes down, spurs in.
- Breastplate, martingale (inoperative from being badly adjusted), dropped noseband, rope noseband.

What is he telling his pony to do?

Fig. 11 The player on the left is sitting back in his saddle, knees out, legs not operating – and his pony is confused. Compare the player on the right: forward on his knees, the pony knows what is wanted, and although the player has a 'flying leg', he is going to get to the ball first.

Fig. 12 This can be described as 'dentistry' – or how to pull out a pony's back teeth! Note the stiff, hollowed back, which has thrown the player out of the saddle; the bit is not acting on the bars of the mouth; the martingale is not operating; and when is the pony going to stop and, if necessary, turn?

Fig. 13 The correct aids for pulling up: seat in the saddle, legs behind the girth (and active); rein hand down, inviting relaxation of the jaw.

with the slightest indication by the rider. This requires suppleness, perfect balance in the saddle and, in a word, horsemanship. Without it, top class as a polo player will be difficult to achieve. But that doesn't mean to say that the game cannot be played and enjoyed by anyone who is prepared to accept the challenge and enjoyment that this supreme game, even at lower levels, can inspire.

Hitting the Ball

All games player know that the art of hitting a ball depends firstly on footwork and secondly on the swing of the object that you are using to try and hit the ball, be it a bat, racket or club. This applies to the polo stick; but 'footwork' in polo depends on the rider, who must control the pony so that he can hit the ball precisely and accurately. The *control* of the pony therefore becomes paramount. That great Jaipur team, mentioned in the Introduction, were indeed a *team* – they were superbly mounted and invariably passed the ball to each other. It is easier said than done. Basically, the rider must control his pony with his knees and lower leg, himself being supple from the hips upwards. There are several reasons for this:

- No relaxation in the control of the pony, even for seconds, is desirable. A jink or swerve at the last moment of hitting the ball may cause a miss.
- The pony must know at all times where the weight of the player is. Flapping legs cause instability, and the habit of throwing the lower leg out when hitting (an Argentine custom) can only confuse and unbalance the pony. Furthermore it can be dangerous. An opponent giving a 'bump' and entangling with an outflying leg, could unhorse the rider with serious consequences. Which does not mean that often the player must not reach for the ball; but his legs must stay 'put'.
- From the point of view of hitting the ball, this should be done from a firm base. This base must be the player, balanced on his

Fig. 14 This is what is apt to happen if you let the outside leg fly out.

Fig. 15 Another example of the flying leg. Note that the player is right out of the saddle.

two knees, supported by his lower legs on the flanks of the pony and his left hand on the pony's withers. Thus can a full shot be made and the player can place his pony as required for the shot. Moreover, the hand on the withers is important. A pony constantly jabbed in the mouth as the result of hitting the ball will, with reason, be disinclined to go to the ball. This applies particularly to a young pony.

- The position in the saddle of a player hence becomes of importance. It will seldom be static. It will all depend on *balance*, in relation to speed. When galloping, balanced forward; to stop and turn, back and firmly in the saddle; hitting, on the knees; but at all times *balanced*. To reiterate, polo is a horseman's

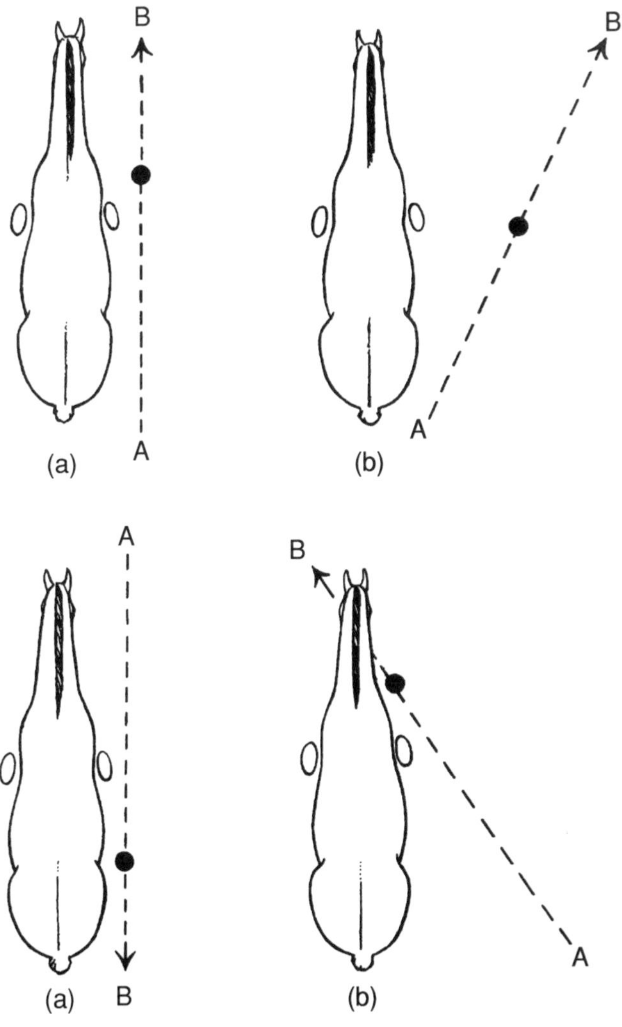

Fig. 16 The ball will generally go in the direction of the plane in which the stick is swung. In the four examples shown, A–B is the plane in which the stick is swung and • is where the ball is hit. In each case, the ball should go towards B.

(a) Offside forehand.
(b) Offside cut-out-shot.
(c) Offside backhander.
(d) Offside under- the-neck shot.

game. The pony must receive the right indications. Above all, rough or hard hands and unnecessary punishment on the mouth will ruin a pony more quickly than anything else.

Stroke Play

- As in any other game in which a bat and ball are involved, the fundamental requirement is to have the correct **swing**. The handle of the polo stick should be held between thumb and forefinger with the end of the stick in the palm of the hand, and the stick swung freely with a supple wrist, as with a squash racquet. The thumb should be passed through the loop at the end of the stick and then passed over the back of the hand. This gives good leverage. The elbow must be kept close into the side and only move, at most, through an arc of about 90° for half shots, or 180° for full shots. The tendency to stick out the elbow merely leads to inaccuracy.
- The ability to hit the ball far is dependent on the speed of the head of the stick, plus weight, at the moment of impact. For instance, the top Indian players used to (perhaps still do) use very whippy sticks. Although small, light men (on the whole), by their perfect timing and through this type of stick, they were able to hit the ball huge distances on hard grounds. *Per contra*, Sinclair Hill, an immensely powerful player, used stiff heavy sticks, and equally was able to hit the ball great distances.
- Swing does not only dictate length, including the ability to tap and control the ball on a bumpy ground, it also controls direction. From this arises the principle that the ball will generally go in the direction of the plane in which the stick is swung. This is illustrated in Fig. 16. In each case A-B is the *plane* in which the stick is swung; • is where the ball is hit. In each case, the ball should go towards B.
- It will be noticed from the diagrams that the ball is hit in a slightly different place in each case. Hence, for accurate striking, it is important to *place* your pony accurately for each shot.
- What applies to offside strokes naturally applies equally to near side ones. But to accomplish these latter with proficiency the player must get well out of the saddle, and over the ball, his

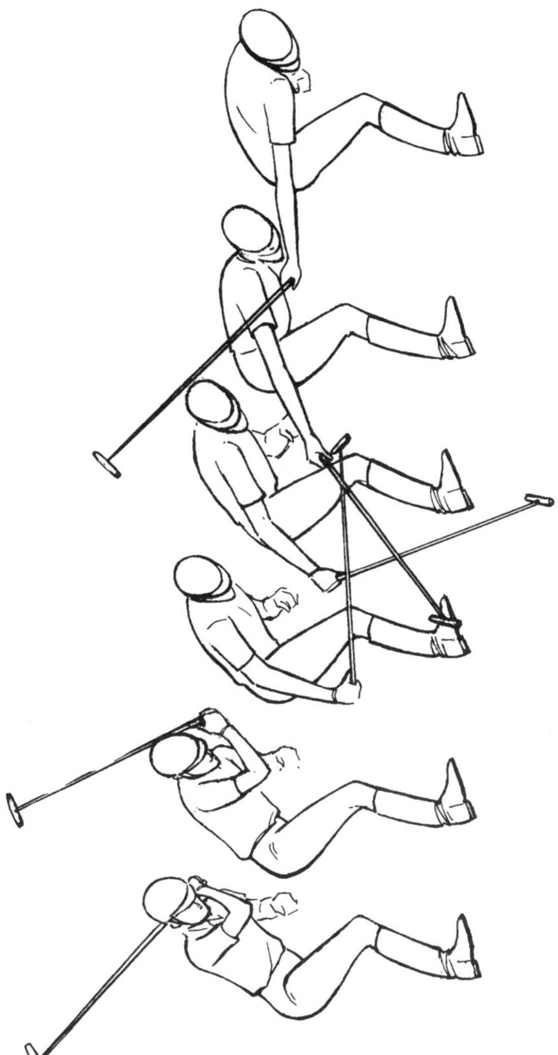

Fig. 17 The offside backhander – like the nearside forehand stroke – is not an easy stroke because (a) it is difficult to get a good swing; and (b) you are hitting only with your thumb behind the stick, instead of with the whole hand. With practice – and if you are not impeded by an opponent in a game – it is possible (and desirable) to swing the stick in a circle with your wrist before striking at the ball. This will give length to your backhander. Illustrated here is the simple backhander. Note that the player's head must be over the ball and the arm should not interfere with the line of sight.

right shoulder pointing approximately between his pony's ears. Considerable suppleness is required, not only in the back and waist, but mainly in the hips.

- For *all* strokes, the player should be out of the saddle, balanced with a 'three-point' suspension, on his knees (but **not** standing in his stirrups), the third point being his left hand on his pony's wither. Thus, he is balanced and can swing freely. Furthermore, he can still use his legs to control and guide his pony, at whatever pace he may be going. In particular, don't sit down for an 'easy' shot in front of goal. That will usually mean a goal missed.
- For forward strokes, the ball should be hit in front of the pony's forelegs; for backhanders, the ball must be hit near the pony's hind legs. Swing and direction have been discussed above.
- At the moment of impact, there should be a straight line from the shoulder, through the arm and the wrist to the stick. But for lift (of the ball) and for distance, the head of the stick should be just in advance of this plumb line at impact.
- A distinguished Indian player from the early part of the century opined that the stick was 'twenty per cent of the game'. He used to visit the ground on the morning of the match, and knowing which ponies he was going to play, and noting the condition of the ground, he would order his sticks to be made up (by his private stick-maker) especially for that match. That does not happen now; but it underscores the principle of the importance of having the right sort of stick. First, the stick should be suitable for the size and strength of the player, in regard to weight and whippiness. Next, it must be of suitable length for the pony being played. It may be remarked here that when playing on soft ground, into which ponies are going to sink, sticks of ½ inch or even 1 inch shorter length are needed. Lastly, the slower the ground, the stiffer the stick. On a wet ground, the ball slows up quickly and shots are often hurried and timing more difficult. On a fast ground, with the ball running on well, there is more time for the shots and a whippier stick can be used.
- Finally, again as in other games, the essence of good stick work is **relaxation**. Tension and a tight grip add up to 'pressing' and poor stroke play. In particular, when hitting in, or taking penal-

ties, the player is recommended when preparing for the stroke to relax his grip altogether momentarily so as to remind himself of the need for a relaxed swing.

5

Ideas on Schooling Polo Ponies

The three main movements to be taught to a polo pony as **specialist** training are:

- To change legs and alter balance at the slightest indication.
- To stop and to start.
- To turn on the haunches (or hocks).

These subjects will be taken in turn, although when schooling, the trainer will integrate them.

To Change Legs and Alter Balance at the Slightest Indication

The pony should be cantered in a circle, to begin with in a large circle. The rider should sit down in the saddle, relax, and try and ride the pony on a loose rein. At this stage, the pony should be ridden in a snaffle with both hands, to make sure that it is 'bent' correctly in the direction it is going. Circle on each rein for about 10 minutes at a time, to get the pony relaxed and going on a loose rein. When changing rein, trot, and do a simple change. When the pony goes quietly in these large circles, smaller circles can be attempted, and eventually figures of eight. The length of time spent on any one rein can be cut down, and more frequent simple changes made. After a period to time (depending on the fitness, balance and intelligence of the pony, and the ability of the rider) the pony will come to understand that on the left rein he leads with his near fore, and vice versa. From here it is a short step to induce a 'flying change' at will.

To achieve a smooth change timing is the essence of the matter, combined with the use of legs and hands. To 'change' a pony from the near to the off fore, wait until the **near fore** hits the ground; then just touch the pony's mouth so as to slightly raise his head and his forehand, and, feeling the right rein, exert pressure with the left leg and put weight on the left seat bone. The pony should change. It may happen that he will not change behind and become disunited. In that case, pull up to a trot and start again. It may also be that, to begin with, you will have to use your left leg more strongly and put more weight on your left seat bone, so as to drive the pony forward and, as it were, away from you. Do not lean forward and look down when executing a change. But as training progresses your pony should change when you use your outside leg and lean your body in the direction required. This should all be done on a loose rein, with the rider sitting pretty deep in the saddle. At about this stage, the pony may have either a double bridle or pelham in its mouth and should be ridden with one hand, using the indirect rein.

The polo pony's ability to change legs at the slightest indication is an absolute requirement. Without it, the pony will not be balanced at all times, and hence unable to accomplish the fast changes in pace and direction needed in the game of polo.

To Stop and to Start

This is arduous work for the pony, particularly a young, green pony. Start at the walk, and when you give the aids to halt (strongly use the legs, and lightly raise the forehand with as light a hand as possible) try and make the pony **draw up** to a halt; **rein-back** three or four paces. Again insist that this is a correct rein-back, with the jaw relaxed, using the loins, and **not** with the head up and the back hollowed. When you can feel the pony is balanced under you, with the hocks beneath him, use your legs again, and by leaning forward a little and taking your weight off his loins, ask him to go forward.

Once the pony understands your aids, and knows what you are asking him to do, the exercise can be done from faster paces. But it will take time to develop the muscles in the loins, quarters and the hind legs, so that the pony does it smoothly, with a relaxed jaw and a rounded back on each occasion (see Fig. 13, p.34).

Do not fall into the error, when stopping, of pushing your legs forward, and pulling on the reins, with your body back and your legs braced against the stirrup leathers. To do this is a certain method of making a pony run away. You are merely pulling against the pony's mouth, and the pony is bound to win. The correct aids are: **first** sit down in the saddle, and at the same time apply your legs strongly behind the girth; then use your hand(s) with the minimum strength required for the occasion.

Naturally, these correct riding-school aids are apt to go by the board in a game. But if you school your pony correctly, it will respond correctly in a game, probably whatever aid you use. Periodically, after a good many games, it will need to be reschooled correctly, so as to eradicate any bad habits it may have acquired.

To Turn on the Haunches (or Hocks)

This also is a very onerous exercise and should not be attempted until other stages of training are well advanced and the pony is well muscled.

What you require the pony to do is to canter (later gallop) in a straight line, turn 180° on the hocks, and canter straight back again after the turn.

It is best to use a fence line, beside which the going is good, to assist in this exercise, and, once again, start teaching the pony from a walk. Approach the fence line at an angle of 45°, and when the pony's head is close to it, halt and turn inwards (Fig. 18). Use the outside leg, free the pony's loins, and give a slight indication

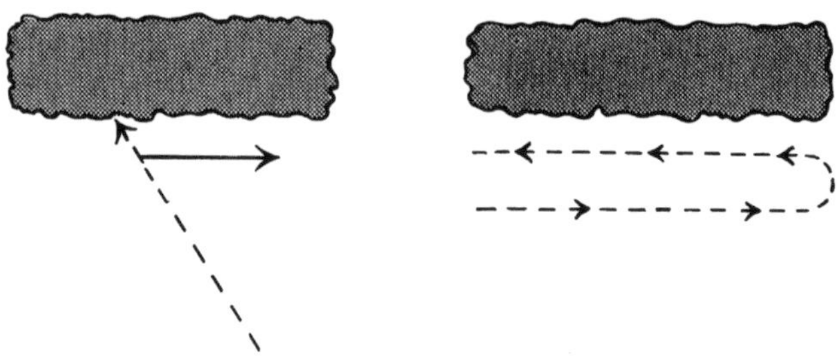

Fig. 18 Exercise for learning to turn on the haunches (see text).

with the inside rein. The inside hind foot, in a perfect turn, should make a complete circle; but do not expect this in the early stages. Do not do this exercise too often at one time; nevertheless progress normally from trot to canter. Keep approaching the fence line at an angle, and make sure that the pony stops correctly, on a straight line, before you ask it to turn. When it is quite proficient in these turns – done, of course, in both directions – then you can canter straight down the fence line, parallel to it and about one and half lengths away from it, and ask your pony to do a complete 180° turn (Fig. 18).

Once you have sat down and halted the pony, the turn should be done by indications from the legs and the weight of the body, on a loose rein.

Too often these days, the necessary time is not spent to allow the pony to mature and gain strength to be able to carry out these arduous exercises. The almost universal use nowadays of the gag-snaffle also obviates the need to teach the pony to bend and flex his jaw, an exercise which requires **time**.

Introducing the Pony to Stick and Ball

It is not advisable to attempt to hit a ball off the pony until its specialist training is fairly well advanced. It should be under full control before you do so. Nevertheless, from early days, it is advisable to carry a polo stick. At first, just carry it; then progress to swinging it very gently through about 90° close to the ground. Only very slowly, whilst soothing the pony with a quiet voice, should the stick be taken past its eye for the first time. Fear must be overcome by gentle means and over a period of time. Eventually, the pony's confidence must be such that you can swing the stick right round both sides of the pony; nor should it mind being touched anywhere on its body with the shaft of the stick.

When the stage has been reached that the pony can be introduced to the ball, put polo boots on the forelegs. Then, at a walk, tap a ball away from you, in a circle, i.e. doing a series of 'cut out' shots. Again, this is to ensure that you do not hit the pony's legs either with stick or ball and frighten it at this stage. Soothe the pony all the time with your voice; just tap the ball with short swings, and even if it shies away (or you miss the ball) complete the stroke and continue on the circle. It is best to have several balls on the ground. A determined pony can avoid going near a single ball; but several balls in close proximity will make it more difficult to prevent you hitting one of them.

Patience is needed, and the pony at this stage should be on a low diet and not too fresh. The aim must be to get the pony cantering about, allowing you to hit the ball from either side, and following the ball on a loose rein.

When you have achieved that, the pony is ready to go into a game.

Entering a Pony

The things which frighten a young pony most when starting to play are:

- Meeting other ponies, particularly if they are going fast. To overcome this, get a friend to ride towards you at various paces, until your pony can meet others with confidence.
- Meeting the ball. Best to get someone on his feet to bowl balls at you at various paces and angles, but keep the pony moving forward on each occasion that a ball is bowled.
- Riding off. As in (a), get a friend to help. To begin with, however, ask your friend to let you get your knee in front of his, and make sure your pony 'wins' his first few ride-offs. Most of them enjoy the competition – when winning – and will quickly learn to push for themselves.

These little training details should most certainly be done before the pony is taken into a game. Even then, the confusion and hurly-burly of the game is daunting for the pony the first time or two. If you can get onto the ground to umpire, or just ride about among the players, it will be a great help.

When you start to play, warn the other players that you are on a young pony, that you are not going fast, and ask them not to bump you too hard nor to hit across in front of your pony. There are few players, indeed, who will not respect this request.

You must then concentrate solely on your pony; don't attempt to take a full part in the game. Keep your place, ask your opponent to ride you off gently, and if the ball comes to you, of course hit it. The pre-requisite, naturally, is that the chukka should be listed as a slow one, so that you do not spoil the game for others. Gradually, however, you can increase the pace, and with constant reschooling and gaining experience all the time, only unsoundness can stop the pony gaining its full potential.

It is generally agreed that it takes two years before a polo pony can be termed 'made'.

Some Random Thoughts on Training

To some, two years may seem unacceptably long; to others, to whom the pony is the essence of the game, it is time enjoyably and gainfully spent, despite the many disappointments and setbacks that will assuredly occur. But hard work and patient perseverance will certainly win in the end.

Horace wrote:

Aequam memento
Rebus in Arduis
Servare Mentem

Which roughly translated, means 'Keep calm.'

The best trainer of polo ponies I know said: 'When you reach the stage of wanting to lambast the brute, stop and light a cigarette; and when you have smoked it, start all over again.'

Training polo ponies is certainly not for fools, nor for those without patience and an understanding of animals.

The human brain is far superior to that of a horse, and the trainer must devise his own ways of overcoming difficulties, which will inevitably occur. Like humans, all horses have different characters, phobias, inhibitions and degrees of determination. Perhaps the most important factor to help a trainer is the horse's compulsion to **go home**. Hence, for instance, any difficult movement (e.g. changing legs in the early stages) should be done **towards home**.

The other thing to remember is that a horse does not have an analytical brain; but it has a most prodigious memory. This also can be made to assist the trainer. Happy occasions and movements well done, **should be repeated in the place and in the same conditions**, e.g. Red Rum at Aintree and the old saying 'Horses for courses'. But don't forget, the opposite is equally true.

Bitting

Correct bitting depends more on the rider (or rather the rider's legs and hands) than on the pony's mouth. It is impossible to lay down any rules. But it must be realised that the two important things in a pony's mouth are, first, its tongue, which must be kept **under the bit all the time**; and secondly, the bars of the mouth. If the tongue is drawn back, the bit is likely to come in direct contact with the bars of the mouth, which are then liable at least to be bruised, if not positively cut open. The pain then generated will cause the pony to pull hard, particularly against the side worst damaged, in a mistaken effort to relieve the pain.

Bars of the mouth in polo ponies often become damaged, and not always by bad hands; running into another pony, or being hit by a stick are frequent causes. Thus it is that a pony's mouth should be carefully inspected after every game. A gag snaffle can also cause damage by wrinkling up the inside of the pony's cheek, which, if the molar teeth are at all sharp, will then be painfully cut and, of course, it operates contrarily to the ideal training of the pony.

In both cases, remedial measures must be taken. It is best, though, to try and obviate the damage. To keep down the tongue means, apart from sympathetic use of the hands, that there must be enough room for the tongue between the bars of the mouth, when pressure on the bit is applied. For this reason, I advocate bits with a port in them, as opposed to half-moon bits, mostly associated with half-moon pelhams. On the application of the curb in the latter bits, pressure is applied towards the tip of the tongue, the most sensitive part, which is then withdrawn. On the application of pressure with a port bit, there becomes *more* room for the tongue, and hence less likelihood of it being withdrawn.

To combat the cutting of the inside cheeks of the pony, all those which go in a gag should have their teeth filed regularly, so that there are no sharp edges to cause damage.

It is considered unfortunate that today the almost universal bit is the gag. From a careful study of many photographs, too, it would seem that martingales are poorly adjusted. This means that the pony's head goes sky high, control is minimised, the back is hollowed and handiness is lost. It is the result, of course, of lack of time and horsemanship required in training the pony. Expediency and economic consideration have taken over from the pursuit of perfection.

Artificial Aids

These are spurs, whips, martingales, dropped nosebands and other such devices. All have their uses.

SPURS A well-trained pony does not need the spur. I cannot remember more than a half dozen ponies of all the ones I have ridden and played which did need it. Hence I believe that spurs should only be used for a specific reason by experienced players. Very few players indeed know exactly where their lower leg is all the time during a game, and the irritation caused to a pony by the constant but unconscious use of the spur largely accounts for ponies 'running on'.

Fig. 19 This player is unaware of the use of his spur. The pony seems fully aware and is resenting it. Nor, judging by the stopping aids being used, is it one which needs 'encouragement'. (Drawn from a photograph)

WHIPS It may be personal prejudice, but I am lost without a whip, carried in my left hand. Not that I use it, except very occasionally, to flip the pony down the near shoulder. But it seems to keep the left hand low and in place, and is certainly needed when riding young ponies.

MARTINGALES In polo, these will always be standing. Due to constant change of pace and direction, the player is always 'at' his pony's mouth. The natural evasion of the pony is to stick its head in the air and thus avoid the action of the bit. The standing martingale is thus an *essential* part of polo saddlery.

The correct length of the martingale is important, and may vary between ponies. As a general guide, however, it can be said that the martingale should not allow the pony to get his head higher than when the bit is level with the pommel of the saddle. One hole may make the whole difference.

BREASTPLATES It has been explained that these are essential in order to keep the martingale at the correct tension and the saddle in place. The argument cannot be accurate. The misguided idea comes from the almost universal use of the gag snaffle and the ensuing throwing up of the head when stopping, hence the **tension** on a leather martingale, which may stretch slightly or even break. Hence those modern, cruel **rope** nosebands. The consequence of the gag is hollowing of the back and subsequent comparative loss of control when stopping. Breastplates can certainly have no influence on the position of the saddle – tension on the martingale attached to the girth ensures that; nor can it influence the martingale. But its weight and encumbrance can to some extent impede the pony. Breastplates serve no purpose.

DROPPED NOSEBANDS These are essential, of course, if a gag is the bit used. But an ordinary cavesson noseband, with a standing martingale attached to it, is also needed for play. Nevertheless, a dropped noseband with a snaffle is perhaps the best combination of bit and aid for **preliminary** work and schooling. A loose dropped noseband has a psychological affect on a pony's head carriage; later, when tightened up, it can keep the mouth shut, and the tongue below the bit, hence ensuring more control.

OTHER DEVICES These may have their uses. There are no absolute rules when it comes to riding horses. But simplicity is best and, in my experience, the good ones (ponies and players) do not require abnormal aids.

6

Wintering and Conditioning of Polo Ponies

Wintering Out

After a long polo season there is nothing more recuperative for polo ponies than a winter's freedom at grass. They can relax mentally and physically; the blows and bruises they will certainly have suffered during the season can recover, and sprains and strains can be medicated and given time to heal. In addition, their mouths are spared the incessant contact. The shoes behind are best removed for the winter rest, but it is advisable to keep the forefeet shod. Without shoes forefeet tend to become broken and the walls of the hooves can split in hard weather. When they have to be shod again, this can induce difficulties and delay in getting them back into regular work.

Before being put out to grass and in view of the changed diet, dosing with a mild wormer is desirable.

The feeding value of grass in winter is not high, but providing there is a good sole of sweet upland grasses it will probably not be necessary to supplement their food from the outset. 'Horsesick' land must be avoided at all costs. Clean running water in good quantity is an essential requirement in any field in which animals are to winter. In hard weather, ice must be broken regularly to ensure a constant supply.

For animals at grass a roofed shelter is not a prime necessity. A horse grows a long coat in winter, which, combined with the grease in the skin, largely protects it from wet and cold. The worst enemy, however, is wind, so protection in the form of a thick hedge or wall offering shelter against the prevailing wind is most desirable.

When the grass provides insufficient feed for the animals, and when the weather becomes really cold, their feeding must be supplemented. Hay, of course, is the main requirement and the quality of hay is important. In one of the worst winters remembered, with prolonged snow and ice, it was fortunate that in the previous summer some good hay had been made of upland grasses and *put in a stack.* It matured beautifully and was cut and fed daily to the animals without any corn supplement. They did wonderfully well and came up in excellent condition. Perhaps this was an exceptional bonus. On another occasion the ponies were fed on hay and 2lbs a day of flaked maize and rolled beans (in those days obtainable as a proprietary brand named 'Kositos'). The maize produced fat and the beans energy, with the result that the ponies galloped about (not to the pleasure of the field's owner!) and when they came up they were fat and hard. They needed little conditioning and we had a wonderful season subsequently.

There are, of course, many different forms of feeding suitable to prevalent conditions. The key is constant supervision, to observe how the animals are faring and to take appropriate action to help the bad-doers.

Conditioning

To a horseman, which I suggest most polo players need to be, this is an exciting and the most constructive time of the polo year. There always used to be conflict about when to bring up the ponies, because there was likely to be a clash in stable capacity with tag-end hunters, point-to-pointers and polo ponies. Perhaps – alas! – those days are past. The appropriate time to bring up ponies from grass must depend on individual circumstances and convenience. In general, though, the longer one has to reschool and slowly to condition one's ponies, the better. The earliest date may well be 1 February – and to those dedicated to the game, and to their ponies, this has always seemed the start of the polo season.

The ponies will come up (or should) looking like woolly bears, with long coats, manes and tails – in fact, a groom's despair! The first thing to do is to give them a physic – and this also applies to any animal coming in from overseas. At one time there was much controversy about the efficacy of this. One year, the ponies were not physicked, and not one of them was 'right' for the whole season. After that, all animals were 'physicked' from grass or from abroad, which makes sense if the complete change of diet from one set of dietary circumstances to another is taken into consideration.

While the animals are 'in physic' is the supreme opportunity (whilst they are not feeling too well) to get their trimming done – cut their manes, pull their tails, clip (as is advisable), re-shoe, file their teeth, worm them and generally give the animal back its self-respect, both for itself as well as its owners.

When out of physic, then starts the conditioning: the slow road work, to harden muscles, leg and sinews. Like hunters, this must form the basis of muscling and fitness. If hills and valleys are available, *walking* up steep hills and *trotting* down them is a wonderful help in achieving balance, muscle and a clear wind at the same time.

As fitness is gained, schooling can start. Not, of course, a fast school to begin with; but make sure that the disciplines of halt and start, change of leg, and turn on the hocks are perfectly done at slow paces.

If you have been schooling a young pony through the winter, this is the stage at which it should be able to 'join the string' and can go forward with the others.

It is also a period when faults in older ponies can be corrected. It becomes a matter of equitation – on which polo at its best depends.

For instance, let us say an animal is apt, when stopping, to bounce, and not use its front legs to assist it to stop. Try to find a really steep (and at the time slippery) slope, go down it and half way down, give the aids to 'stop'. The pony will quickly lose its hind legs and will drop its front – perhaps not the first time, but it will be surprising if it does not learn the lesson. Man's brain is infinitely superior to that of a horse, and it is by such simple means, without punishment, that a horse can be made to submit to man's will. There are many other such simple means to overcome these – shall we say – technical failures in a pony's schooling and help it reach its full potential. Do **not**, as was once described to me, try riding the pony at full gallop into a wall to make it stop. I understood that at least one pony was killed this way!

Come warmer weather, rugs can be discarded, the coats will come through, and above all, acquiescence becomes easier to obtain. Then start slow chukkas and old and young ponies can be conditioned to going faster. It is all progressive, but requires patience.

Finally, a word of warning. *Never* let your grooms ride your ponies, either at exercise or to and from the ground, in anything other than a snaffle. Nor should any of them – except experienced and proven horsemen – be allowed to school ponies.

7

Umpiring

Perhaps it should not be so, but polo being a game of speed, contact and instant decision, requires strict control. Umpiring – as in cricket – therefore becomes of supreme importance, not only for the sake of safety, but also to assure the fair result of a game.

The Rules are abundantly clear; they cater for almost every possible situation, and in my time as an umpire, I do not remember a situation which was not covered by the Rules. In the Instructions to Umpires (HPA Year Book), the positioning (all-important) of umpires during the game is clearly indicated.

However, from personal observation, these instructions are not always observed – but they are important, so that umpires can see and assess what is taking place in the game and not interfere with the play. Basically the theory is that the umpires should be echeloned across the ground. By previous agreement, the two umpires each take one side and one back line, thereby dividing the ground diagonally. At half time, sides are changed. From this it is clear that when the ball goes behind, the responsible umpire goes behind his back line and is in a position then to judge the line of the hit-in; or in the case of a 60-yard hit, whatever might go on. In the case of 30- or 40-yard hits, the umpire whose back line it is should be *on* the back line, so as to see that the defending players do not infringe the Rules. The umpire not behind or on the back line positions himself behind the striker in the case of 30- or 40-yard penalties, but on the 30-yard line to one side in the case of a hit-in.

As play develops the umpires automatically then become echeloned and can best, between them, descry the line of the ball, on which all umpiring depends.

It is a mistake to think that one can accurately discern who has the right of way from close-to; the important point is to see what leads up to any potential misdemeanour and to ascertain in a flash who has the Right of Way and thus to be able to decide more accurately whether a foul has been committed or not.

Another important matter for umpires is in relation to Field Rules 4 and 5. Before a match starts it is incumbent on the umpires to see that these two rules are observed. A snap sample inspection of calkins need not take long, and I can remember a pony being disqualified before the game for an offence under these rules. Similarly – and more quickly done – a player's equipment should be scrutinised and the player barred until such time as the offence been removed. Among those things to be observed are:

- Spurs. Few spurs are not sharp and those currently in use – the bronze rollers imported from the Argentine, some of which are serrated and worn on the heel of the boot – would seem to fall into this category.
- Buckles on the outside of the knee or leg.
- Some types of knee pads. Many protrude well beyond the front or side of the knee and are made of hard, reinforced leather. They are of an offensive nature, as opposed to being purely defensive protection and seem not only to prevent close 'riding off', but also, with a good bump, could cause pain and injury to the receiver of the bump.

Perhaps it is time the HPA gave a ruling on these matters.

But apart from all this, good umpires are born and not made. No particular category of polo player can necessarily become a good umpire. High-goal players are often some of the worst; a low-goal player may or may not be good. Ability in umpiring depends on:

- Knowledge of the Rules. This knowledge must be so that he can quote – if asked – the paragraph on which his decision depends. This needs constant study.
- Concentration, on the line of the ball and thus the right of way, and **not** on the players.
- His quickness of mind and eye to evaluate what has been going on, and to blow quickly on infringement.
- His standing, as an umpire, among polo players at all levels,

consequent upon his experience as such. Indeed, he may be retired from playing altogether.

I repeat: as in the making of polo ponies, umpires are born and not made. But don't get it wrong; the umpire will almost always be blackguarded and receive little praise. His only satisfaction is the knowledge that he has done his best and has been impartial. But pleasure will be gained just by being on the ground during a match of the best and fastest game in the world – polo.

8
For Beginners

Getting Started

As has been stressed, the essence – indeed a *sine qua non* – for aspiring polo players is **horsemanship**. Nowadays the Pony Club undertake riding instruction for the young and Pony Club polo is booming. It is greatly encouraging to learn the numbers that now participate. But to enhance their horsemanship, it would seem desirable during the Christmas and Easter breaks for courses to be arranged for selected *male* youngsters with the Household Cavalry, Kings Troop, RHA, and/or Imber Court in horsemanship and horsemastership. Nothing to do with polo; just strengthen their 'seats'. Males are singled out here because although young females may well be better in their 'teens' than young males, in maturity females just do not have the strength to achieve other than a minor handicap and they have never been strong enough to take on the males in a good fast game.

▪ Hitting the ball and learning the game come from **practice** and **hardwork** – which is not unenjoyable in itself. It is a matter of opportunity and determination, plus the backing of kind parents or sponsors to stand behind the inevitable expense of mounting the aspirant.

▪ The next problem is **where to play** and **where to learn**. The aspirant should first of all arm himself with the current Hurlingham Polo Association Year Book, published annually and obtainable from the Honorary Secretary of the HPA, Winterlake,

Fig. 20 A well turned-out player and pony. Note: (a) the well-adjusted martingale; (b) boots and bandages on all four legs; (c) coronet guards; (d) no spurs.

Kirtlington, Oxford, OX5 3HG (Tel: 0869 50044). This gives comprehensive information on all Polo Clubs in England (and abroad) and their officials; incorporates the Rules (which must be read carefully by all aspirants); and lists all players and their handicaps. It is a **must** for all young (and old) players.

■ There is an obvious attraction to play at Cowdray, Windsor or Cirencester. These are the big clubs where the highest class polo is played. But the beginner should be more modest, and try to join and learn the ropes from smaller country clubs – such as Kirtlington, Tidworth, Offchurch, Toulston and many similar, where polo is played for fun! He will find the polo more enjoyable and will consequently learn more. When he has served his 'apprenticeship' (it was always said it takes ten years to make a player and two to make a pony), if he is good enough and is well mounted he will find himself playing in the best company at the centres of the best polo. Be assured of that.

■ As regard **instruction in polo**, the best answer is to apply to the Polo Manager of the club most conveniently placed where you wish to start. He can also give advice on where to buy the necessary kit and who is likely to have suitable ponies for sale.

Equipment and Dress

As regards the **kit** necessary, it is axiomatic that firms purveying polo equipment will attempt to sell as much as possible. The absolute essentials are: helmet (but *without* visor); sticks – (see Chapter 6) but note, stiffish sticks suit beginners best; polo boots (without buckles on the outside); breeches (washable); a long polo whip; and a couple of vests, one white and one red. Also recommended is a string glove for the left hand. On occasions, when playing in rain, a thin cotton glove on the right hand will prevent the stick handle slipping in your hand. Padded knee pads, a helmet visor, spurs or other impedimenta are not recommended.

Unless he is playing on hired ponies, the young player will also need to equip his ponies. Each should have, of course, a complete saddle, standing martingale, boots (preferable) or bandages for each leg, as well as normal stable equipment, such as headcollars, grooming kit, sponges, buckets, etc. On the ground, the pony will need attention after each chukka. A canvas bucket is recommended (easily transported) together with sponges, **rubber** sweat scrapers and chamois leathers for drying off after washing down. Lastly, some form of thin rug covering is most desirable, indeed on certain occasions essential when a cold wind is blowing, to cover each animal while cooling off.

I have omitted one thing – bridles, but see Chapter 5 above. If he is wise, a young player will collect different sorts of bits, some conventional, and some more severe. Changing bits around in a pony's mouth somehow 'freshens' it and one can find, by experience, which bit suits a pony best, and in which it goes most happily. After all, some people prefer gin to whisky, or cider to beer! Likewise a pony with bits.

It must be remembered that the good polo pony is a very sensitive animal and one must pander to its whims and try to bring it onto the ground in the best possible frame of mind, especially for an important match. Then it has to be looked after between chukkas. When asked about this recently, one dedicated lady groom said: 'Of course we do (this and that); after all, *no ponies, no polo*.'

General Rules of Polo

As published by The Hurlingham Polo Association and printed here by their kind permission.

HEIGHT OF PONIES

1–Ponies of any height may be played.

SIZE OF GROUNDS

2–(a) A full-sized ground shall not exceed 300 yards in length by 200 yards in width, if unboarded; and 300 yards in length by 160 yards in width, if boarded.

(b) The goals shall not be less than 250 yards apart, and each goal shall be 8 yards wide.

(c) The goal posts shall be at least 10 feet high, and light enough to break if collided with.

(d) The boards shall not exceed 11 inches in height.

SIZE OF BALL

3–The size of the ball shall not exceed 3½ inches in diameter, and the weight of the ball shall be within the limits of 4¼ to 4¾ ounces.

QUALIFICATIONS OF PLAYERS

4–(a) The number of players is limited to four a side in all games and matches.

(b) No player may play under the influence of stimulative drugs.

(c) No player shall play with his left hand.

Note 1: No person shall play in any tournament or advertised match conducted by an Affiliated club or Association in the British Isles unless:

(i) He is an Associate Member of the HPA.

(ii) He has lodged a signed declaration either with his Club or the HPA, to be bound by the rules, regulations, orders and directives of the HPA.

(iii) He is listed in the Association's current handicap list,
or has been allotted a handicap by the Association's Handicap Committee during the current season,
or his handicap has been confirmed by the Honorary Secretary of the Association.

Note 2: Please refer to the Rules for Official Tournaments, obtainable from the HPA.

SUBSTITUTION

5–(a) A player may only play in one team in the same tournament and in a tournament with the same 'control number' in the fixture list, **unless he has been knocked out of the latter tournament and is not due to play any further matches therein**, except as stated in (e) below.

(b) Substitutes must be qualified to play in the tournament and the team must remain qualified after the substitution has been made.

(c) A player who has taken part in one or more of the earlier rounds of a tournament, who is unable to play in a later round or rounds, may be replaced by a substitute. A member of a team who is unable to play in the earlier rounds of a tournament may also be replaced by a substitute.

(d) A player may be substituted for another during a match only if the latter player through sickness, accident or duty is unable to continue. If the substitute is of the same or lower handicap the score will not be altered, however if he is of a higher handicap the score will be immediately altered to reflect the increased aggregate handicap of the side irrespective of the period of play in which the substitution occurred.

(e) A Tournament Committee may agree to **any** player being used as a substitute provided:

(i) They consider there is no suitable player (see Note 1)

available who has not already played in the tournament or has been knocked out of a tournament with the same control number and is not due to play any further matches therein.

(ii) They are satisfied that there is a bona fide need for a substitute.

(iii) The total handicap of the team requiring a substitute will not be increased thereby, except in the circumstances described in (d) above. If a second substitute is brought into a team, it shall be the handicap the last time the team played which shall count.

(iv) In matches with an International flavour the captain of the opposing team's side agrees.

Notes on Substitution Rules

(1) A player shall be regarded as 'suitable' if his handicap is not more than two goals less than the handicap of the player he is replacing.

(2) If a player is brought in, in the case of an emergency for the completion of one match, he shall not be disqualified from continuing with his original team nor from joining another team if he is not already in one; he may continue to play with that team provided the original player is still not available and his own team is not still in the tournament.

(3) If a player is late and the game is started with a substitute, the late player may replace the substitute after the first chukka, but not thereafter.

(4) In the prospectus of a tournament with a subsidiary, it should be clearly stated whether or not both count as one tournament for the purposes of these rules.

QUALIFICATIONS OF PONIES

6–(i) Ponies of any height may be played.

(ii) A pony blind in one eye may not be played (see Field Rule 3).

(iii) A pony may not be played which is not under proper control (see Field Rule 3).

(iv) In high- and medium-goal tournaments, a pony played by one team cannot be played by any other team in the same tournament.

Notes:

(1) Attention is drawn to the Directive on the Misuse of Drugs and the Welfare of Ponies (details given in the HPA Yearbook).

(2) In the British Isles all polo ponies must have a current certificate of vaccination.

UMPIRES, REFEREES AND GOAL JUDGES

7–(a) The Rules shall be administered in a match by two Umpires, who shall be mounted to enable them to keep close to the play, and a Referee who shall remain off the field of play in a central position. By mutual agreement between Captains of teams, one Umpire and if desired, also the Referee, may be dispensed with. The decision of the Umpire shall be final, except where there are two and they disagree, in which case the decision of the Referee shall be final.

(b) In important matches Goal Judges shall be appointed each of whom shall give testimony to the Umpires at the latters' request in respect to goals or other points of the game near his goal, but the Umpires shall make all decisions.

(c) The above Officials shall be nominated by the Committee conducting the tournament or match except in international matches when they shall be mutually agreed upon.

(d) **No player shall appeal in any manner to the umpire or umpires for fouls, nor may they discuss or dispute a decision with the umpire or umpires during the game, except that the captain has the sole right to ask for clarification on a decision.**

(e) **The referee and umpires must discuss the conduct of the game at half-time.**

(f) The Authority of the above Officials shall extend from the time the match is due to start until the end of the game. All questions arising at other times may be referred by the Captains to the Committee conducting the tournament or match and its decision shall be final.

Note: In the British Isles, except in International matches, every possible effort will be made to appoint at least one British Umpire. It is recommended that the referee is also British, and should be a regular past or present player in polo at least to the level being refereed.

TIMEKEEPER AND SCORER

8–An official Timekeeper and Scorer shall be employed in all games and matches.

DOCTORS AND VETERINARIANS

9–At all organised polo games there will be a doctor and/or para-medic with NHS or equivalent qualifications, and a veterinary surgeon either present or on immediate call. A wagon equipped with screen must also be provided.

Should the umpire require medical assistance for an injured player, he should signal by waving his stick above his head.

DURATION OF PLAY

10–(a) The duration of play is forty-two minutes divided into six periods of seven minutes each. The number of minutes played in a period, or periods played in a match, may be reduced by the Committee conducting the tournament or match. In all matches there shall be a half-time interval of five minutes. All other intervals between periods shall be of three minutes' duration.

HANDICAP CALCULATION

(b) In all matches played under handicap conditions the higher handicapped team shall concede to the lower handicapped team the difference in the handicaps divided by six and multiplied by the number of periods of play of the match. All fractions of a goal shall count as 'half-a-goal'. Mistakes in handicaps or in computing goal allowances must be challenged before a match begins, and no objection can be entertained afterwards.

PLAY CONTINUOUS

(c) With the exception of the said intervals, play shall be continuous, and no time shall be taken off for changing ponies during a period, except as legislated for in Field Rule 23.

TERMINATION OF PERIOD

(d) Each period of play, except the last, shall terminate after the expiration of the prescribed time (designated by the ringing of the bell or other signal) as soon as the ball goes out of play or hits the boards.

A bell or other signal will be sounded thirty seconds after the first bell or signal, if the ball is still in play, and the period will terminate at the first sound of the second bell or other signal, although the ball is still in play, wherever the ball may be, even if the umpires fail to hear the bell or signal.

PENALTY EXACTED NEXT PERIOD

(e) If a foul is given after the first stroke of the seven-minute bell, the Umpire's whistle terminates the period, and the penalty shall be exacted at the beginning of the next period, except in the event of a tie in the last period when the penalty shall be exacted at once, and the period continued until the ball goes out of play or hits the boards or the thirty-seconds bell is sounded.

GAME STOPPED

(f) The game can be stopped in two different ways:

(i) Where the time during which the game is stopped is *not* to be counted as part of the playing time of the period (i.e. where the clock is to be stopped). To indicate this to the Timekeeper the Umpire should blow one firm blast. This way is used for fouls, Penalty 7 and under Field Rules 11, 14, 21 and 23. The ball is dead until the Umpire says 'Play', and the ball is hit or hit at.

(ii) Where the time during which the game is stopped is to be counted as part of the playing time of the period (i.e. where the clock is *not* to be stopped). This occurs when the ball goes out of play, through the goal or over the boards, side or back lines (unless hit over the back line by a defender). As a rule the game will automatically stop, but if it continues (e.g. if the ball is hit straight into play after crossing the back or side lines), the Umpire should blow two sharp blasts. This will tell the Timekeeper not to deduct time.

LAST PERIOD

(g) The last period shall terminate although the ball is still in play, at the first stroke of the seven-minute bell, wherever the ball may be, except in the case of a tie.

(h) In the case of a tie the last period shall be prolonged till the ball goes out of play or hits the boards, or till the thirty-seconds bell rings, and if still a tie, after an interval of five minutes the game shall be started from where the ball went out of play and be continued in periods of the usual duration, with the usual intervals, until one side obtains a goal, which shall determine the match.

WIDENED GOALS

(i) In the event of a tie at the end of the final period of a match goals will be widened for the ensuing periods:

- (a) If the tournament conditions state that this will be so, or
- (b) If the captains of both teams concerned request that they should be.

In any event goals will be widened if no goal has been scored by the end of the first period of extra time.

Rules for Widened Goals:

- (i) Width of goals to be doubled to 16 yards by moving goal posts 4 yards outwards.
- (ii) After a five minutes' interval ends shall be changed and the ball thrown in from the centre in the first of the extra chukkas.

Note: Committees are advised to put in the sockets to hold the goal posts at the 4-yard extensions before the tournament begins.

PROLONGATION IN CASE OF PENALTY

(j) In the event of a penalty being awarded within twenty seconds of the end of the match, the Timekeeper shall allow twenty seconds play from the time the ball is hit, or hit at, in carrying out the penalty, before he rings the final (seven-minute) bell. If a goal is scored after the ball has been put into play, the final bell shall be rung, if the original regular time (seven-minutes) has expired. The match shall terminate as usual on the first stroke of the final (seven-minute) bell.

UNFINISHED MATCH

(k) Once a match has started it shall be played to a finish

unless stopped by the Umpire for some unavoidable cause, which prevents a finish the same day, such as darkness or the weather, in which case it shall be resumed at the point at which it has stopped, as to score, period and position of the ball, at the earliest convenient time, to be decided upon by the Committee conducting the tournament.

HOW GAME IS WON

11–The side that scores most goals wins the game.

POLO HELMET OR CAP

12–No one shall be allowed to **play or umpire** unless he wears a protective polo helmet or polo cap, either of which must be worn with a chin strap.

CONFUSING COLOURS

13–If in the opinion of the Tournament Committee the colours of two competing teams are so alike as to lead to confusion, the team lower in the draw or second named in a league competition shall be instructed to play in some other colours.

Field Rules

DEFINITION OF FOUL

1–Any infringement of the Field Rules constitutes a foul and the Umpire may stop the game.

DEAD BALL

2–The Umpire shall carry a whistle, which he shall blow when he wishes to stop the game. When he does so the ball is dead until he says 'Play', and the time is dead and not counted in the playing time of the period, except as legislated for in General Rule 10 (f).

Note: If a whistle is blown for a foul at approximately the same time as a goal is scored:

(i) The goal will be disallowed if the foul was against the attacking side and the foul was confirmed.

(ii) The goal will be allowed if the foul was against the attacking side and the foul is over-ruled; or if the foul was against the defending side whether or not the foul is confirmed.

DISQUALIFIED PONIES

3–A pony blind of an eye may not be played; a pony showing vice, or not under proper control, shall not be allowed in the game.

Note: In the British Isles all polo ponies must have a current certificate of flu vaccination.

EQUIPMENT FOR PONIES

4–(a) Protection of ponies by boots or bandages on all four legs is compulsory.

(b) Blinkers are not allowed, nor any form of noseband which obstructs the vision.

(c) Rimmed shoes are allowed, but the rim may only be on the inside of the shoe.

(d) Road studs, frost nails, screws and fancy shaped spikes are not allowed. If a shoe has a calkin or fixed stud it must only be on the outside heel of the hind shoe and it must be balanced by a raised, sloping and feathered inside heel. The best stud is the removable stud, which must only be on the outside heel of the hind shoe; it must not have a hard core like a road stud; it should always be removed before the pony leaves the polo grounds. The size of a calkin or stud must not be more than a half inch cube.

(e) Hackamores or bitless bridles will not be used in matches or tournaments.

(f) Umpires' ponies must be equipped as for polo except that their tails need not to be put up.

Note: The movable calkin is allowed so that when it becomes worn it can be replaced by a fresh one without re-shoeing. The essence of this permission is that the movable calkin should resemble, as far as possible, the recognised form of fixed calkin, and it does not permit the fixing of any fancy shaped spike, nor the placing of the calkin anywhere except at the heels of the hind shoes.

DISQUALIFIED EQUIPMENT FOR PLAYERS

5–(a) Sharp spurs are not allowed.

(b) No player may wear buckles or studs on the upper part of his polo boots or knee pads in such a way as could damage another player's boots or breeches.

(c) Whips must not be more than 48 inches long, including any tag.

SAFETY ZONE

6–(a) No person is allowed on the ground during play for any purpose whatever except the players and the Umpires. A player requiring a stick, pony or other assistance from an outside person must ride to the boards, side or back lines, to procure it. No person may come on to the ground to assist him.

(b) No person or pony is allowed within the safety zone during play except those playing, umpires, referee, goal judges, manager and stickholders.

Note: The Safety Zone is an area including the field of play, the ground within about 10 yards of the boards and the ground within about 30 yards of the goal line.

START OF GAME

7–At the beginning of the game the two teams shall line up in the middle of the ground, each team being on its own side of the half-way line. The Umpire shall bowl the ball underhand and hard between the opposing ranks of players, from a distance of not less than five yards, the players remaining stationary until the ball has left his hand.

HOW A GOAL IS SCORED

8–A goal is scored when a ball passes between the goal posts and over and clear of the goal line. If a ball is hit above the top of the goal posts, but in the opinion of the Umpire between those posts produced, it shall count as a goal.

CHANGING OF ENDS

9–(a) Ends shall be changed after every goal except where a goal is awarded under Penalty 1. Ends shall also be changed if no goals have been hit by half-time (in a seven or five period match, after the fourth or third period respectively), and play shall be re-started at a position corresponding to the change of ends. After a goal has been hit, the game shall be re-started from the middle of the ground as prescribed by Field Rule 7. The players shall be allowed a reasonable time in which to reach the middle of the ground at a slow trot and take up their positions.

WRONG LINE-UP

(b) If the Umpire inadvertently permits lining up the wrong way the responsibility rests with him, and there is no redress; but if at the end of the period no goal has been scored the ends shall then be changed.

ATTACKERS HIT BEHIND

10–(a) The ball must go over and be clear of the back line to be out.

(b) When the ball is hit behind the back line by the attacking side, it shall be hit in by the defenders from the spot where it crossed the line, but at least four yards from the goal posts or boards, when the umpire **calls** 'Play'. None of the attacking side shall be within 30 yards of the back line until the ball is hit or hit at; the defenders being free to place themselves where they choose.

(c) The defenders shall give the attacking side reasonable time to get into position, but there shall be no unnecessary delay in hitting in. In the event of unnecessary delay the Umpires shall call on the offending side to hit in at once. If the Umpire's request is not complied with, he shall **throw** in the ball underhand and hard, at the spot where the ball crossed the back line and at right angles to it. **For such a throw in, the team which delayed play shall be on the side nearest the goal**.

DEFENDERS HIT BEHIND

11–If the ball be hit behind the back line by one of the defending side, either directly or after glancing off his own pony, or after glancing off the side boards, Penalty 6 shall be exacted. If the ball strikes any other player or his pony before going behind, it shall be hit in in accordance with Field Rule 10.

BALL HIT OUT

12–(a) The ball must go over and clear the side lines or boards to be out.

(b) When the ball is hit over the boards or side line, it must be bowled, underhand and hard, by the Umpire into the ground from a point just inside the boards or lines where it went out, on an imaginary line parallel to the two goal lines, and between the opposing ranks of players, each side being on its own side of the imaginary line. No player may stand within 10 yards of the side lines or boards. Players must remain stationary until the ball has left the Umpire's hand. A reasonable time must be allowed players in which to line up.

RESTARTING AFTER INTERVAL

13–On play being resumed after an interval, the ball shall be put in play in the normal manner which would have been followed had there been no interval, i.e. in accordance with Field Rules 9, 10, 12 or 26, as the case may be. If the ball hits the side boards without going over them at the end of the previous period, it shall be treated as though it had been hit over them as laid down in Field Rule 12. The Umpire must not wait for players who are late.

Note: General rule 10 (e) deals with resuming play when a period ends with a foul.

DAMAGED BALL

14–If the ball be damaged or trodden into the ground, the Umpire shall, at his discretion, stop the game and re-start it with a new ball, in the manner prescribed in Field Rule 26.

Note: It is desirable that the game shall be stopped and the ball changed when the damaged ball is in such a position that neither side is favoured thereby.

CARRYING THE BALL

15–A player may not catch, kick or hit the ball with anything but his stick.He may block with any part of his body but not with an open hand. He may not carry the ball intentionally. If the ball becomes lodged against a player, his pony or its equipment, in such a way that it cannot be dropped immediately, the Umpire shall blow his whistle and restart the game in accordance with Field Rule 26 at the point where it was first carried.

CROSSING

16–THE RIGHT OF WAY

(a) (i) At each moment of the game there shall exist a Right of Way, which shall be considered to extend ahead of the player entitled to it, and in the direction in which he is riding.

No player shall enter or cross this Right of Way except at such a distance that not the slightest risk of a collision or danger to either player is involved.
(See *Rules Appendix*, Example II.)

(a) (ii) The Right of Way, which is defined in paras (c) to (e) below, is not to be confused with the line of the ball and does not depend on who last hit it.

The Line of the Ball

(b) (i) The line of the ball is the line of its course or that line produced at any moment.

(b) (ii) If the line of the ball changes unexpectedly, for example when a ball glances off a pony, and as a result the Right of Way changes, the player who had the Right of Way must be given room to continue a short distance on his original Right of Way.

(b) (iii) When a dead ball has been put into play through being hit at and missed the line of the ball is considered to be the direction in which the player was riding when he hit at it.

(b) (iv) If the ball becomes stationary while remaining in play, the line of the ball is that line upon which it was travelling before stopping.

Player riding in direction ball is travelling

(c) (i) A player following the ball on its exact line and taking it on his offside, is entitled to the Right of Way over all other players. (See *Rules Appendix*, Example II.)

(c) (ii) Where no player is riding on the exact line of the ball, the Right of Way belongs to the player following it on the smallest angle, provided he does not contravene Clause (f). (See *Rules Appendix*, Example V.)

(c) (iii) Two players when following the exact line of the ball attempting to ride one another off, share the Right of Way over all other players. (See *Rules Appendix*, Example IV.)

(c) (iv) A player riding in the direction the ball is travelling at an angle to its line, has the Right of Way over a player riding to meet the ball at an angle to its line, irrespective of the width of the angle provided he does not contravene Clause (f). (See *Rules Appendix*, Example I.)

(c) (v) No player shall be deemed to have the Right of Way by reason of his being the last striker if he shall have deviated from pursuing the exact line of the ball. (See *Rules Appendix*, Example VI.)

Equal Angles

(d) In the rare case of two players riding in the general direction of the ball at exactly equal angles to it on opposite sides of its line, the Right of Way belongs to that player who has the line of the ball on his offside. The same rule applies as between players meeting the ball at exactly equal angles from opposite sides of its line.

Player meeting the ball

(e) (i) A player who rides to meet the ball on its exact line has the Right of Way over all players riding at an angle from any direction. (See *Rules Appendix*, Example III.)

(e) (ii) As between players riding to meet the ball, that player has the Right of Way whose course is at the least angle to the line of the ball.

Player to take ball on offside

(f) The Right of Way entitles a player to take the ball on the offside of his pony. If he places himself to hit it on the near side and thereby in any way endangers another player who would otherwise have been clear, he loses the Right of Way and must give way to this other player. (See *Rules Appendix*, Example I.)

(g) When two players are riding from exactly opposite directions to hit the ball each shall take it on the offside of his pony. If a collision appears probable the player who has the Right of Way must be given way to. (See *Rules Appendix*, Example I and III.)

Checking

(h) (i) No player may check or pull up either on or across the

Right of Way if by so doing he runs the slightest risk of collision with the player entitled to it.

(h) (ii) If a player enters safely on the Right of Way and does not check, a player must not ride into him from behind, but must take the ball on the nearside of his own pony.

(h) (iii) If a player with possession of the ball or right to the line of the ball on his off-side, checks his speed to such an extent that an opposing player may enter the line and take the ball on his off-side, without, in the opinion of the umpires, creating any danger to the checking player, if that player were to *maintain* his reduced speed, then no foul shall be deemed to have occurred, even if the checking player subsequently increases his speed. Umpires are advised that if the checking player slows to a walk or stops completely, under this directive, it is almost impossible for any danger to occur and therefore no foul is committed.

DANGEROUS RIDING

17–A player may ride off an opponent, but he may not ride dangerously, as for example:

(a) Bumping at an angle dangerous to a player, or his pony.

(b) Zigzagging in front of another player riding at a gallop, in such a way as to cause the latter to check his pace or risk a fall.

(c) Pulling across or over a pony's legs in such a manner as to risk tripping the pony, etc.

(d) Riding an opponent across the Right of Way. (See *Rules Appendix*, Example VII.)

(e) Riding at an opponent in such a manner as to intimidate and cause him to pull out or miss his stroke, although no foul or cross actually occurs.

(f) 'Sandwiching', i.e. two players of the same team riding off an opponent at the same time.

(g) **Deliberately riding one's mount into the stroke of another player.***

* *Note to Rule 17(g)* The rules gives the Umpire the opportunity to call a foul on either the player striking the ball or the opponent riding into play. If, in the opinion of the Umpire, the player striking the ball started the stroke while clear of an opponent's mount, but did in fact hit into the legs of an opponent as a result of the opponent riding into the stroke, then no foul is called on the player hitting the (continued on next page)

USE OF THE WHIP AND SPURS

18–The whip and/or spurs may not be used unnecessarily or excessively. In the course of matches and chukkas, polo clubs must ensure that, save exceptional circumstances, whips must not be used to strike ponies except on the ground when the ball is in play.

ROUGH HANDLING

19–No player shall seize with the hand, strike, or push with the head, hand, forearm or elbow, but a player may push with his arm, above the elbow, provided the elbow be kept close to the side.

MISUSE OF STICK

20–(a) No player may hook an opponent's stick, unless he is on the same side of the opponent's pony as the ball, or in a direct line behind, and his stick is neither over or under the body or across the legs of an opponent's pony, nor may any player hook or strike at an opponent's stick unless all of the opponent's stick is below the opponent's shoulder level. The stick may not be hooked or struck unless the opponent is in the act of striking the ball.

(b) No player may reach immediately over and across or under and across any part of an opponent's pony to strike at the ball, nor may he hit into or amongst the legs of an opponent's pony.

(c) No player may intentionally strike his pony with his polo stick.

(d) No player may use his stick dangerously, or hold it in such a way as to interfere with another player or his pony.

(Note to rule 17g cont.) ball. Furthermore, if, in the opinion of the Umpire, the opponent dangerously rode into the stroke of the player on the ball, the Umpire may call a foul on the opponent. By the same standard, if the player of the ball dangerously strikes into the mount of an opponent who was alongside when the player began the stroke, the striker may be called for a foul.

Two situations where the Umpire would usually call a foul on the opponent for riding into the player's ongoing swing are: (1) where the opponent's mount is endangered by causing it to be struck by the player's stick, and (2) where the opponent endangers a player who is leaning way out making a shot (usually, but not necessarily, a back shot) by riding up fast from behind at the last minute between the ball and the mount of the player making the shot causing the player making the shot to be hit from behind by the head of the opponent's mount.

(e) No player may knowingly strike the ball after the whistle.

Note: If a hit occurs after the whistle for a foul, the Umpire may increase the severity of the penalty if the hit is by a member of the fouling team, or cancel the penalty or decrease its severity if the hit is by a member of the team fouled.

LOSS OF HEADGEAR

21–If a player loses his headgear the Umpire shall stop the game to enable him to recover it, but not until an opportunity occurs that neither side is favoured thereby.

DISMOUNTED PLAYER

22–No dismounted player may hit the ball or interfere in the game.

ACCIDENT OR INJURY

23–(a) If a pony falls or goes lame, or if a player or pony be injured, or in the case of an accident to a pony's gear which in the opinion of the Umpire involves danger to the players or other ponies, the Umpire shall stop the game.

(b) If a player falls off his pony, the Umpire shall not stop the game, **until the ball is in a neutral position**, unless he is of the opinion that the player is injured or is **liable to be injured**. What constitutes a fall is left to the decision of the Umpire.

(c) When the game has been stopped in accordance with Clause (a) above, the Umpire shall re-start the game in the manner laid down in Field Rule 26, directly the player concerned is ready to resume play. The Umpire shall not wait for any other player who may not be present.

(d) If a player be injured, a period not exceeding fifteen minutes shall be allowed for his recovery. If the injured player is unfit to play after fifteen minutes, the game shall be restarted with a substitute in place of the injured player, unless Penalty 8 has been exacted. If, however, the injured player subsequently recovers he may replace the player who was substituted in his place, but the handicap of the higher handicapped player will be counted in accordance with General Rule 5 (d).

(e) In the event of a player being, or seeming to be, concussed, the following action will be taken. The umpires, or if no umpires are present, the senior player on the ground will stop the game and arrange for the player to see a doctor as soon as possible. The player will not be permitted to play again for a minimum of one week without a certificate of fitness from the official medical officer of his club. If no doctor is present when the accident occurred it will be the sole responsibility of the umpires or the senior player present to decide if the player was actually concussed.

DISABLEMENT

24–If a player be disabled by a foul so that he is unable to continue, Penalty 8 may be exacted, or the side which has been fouled shall have the option of providing a substitute. Penalty 1, 2 or 3 shall be exacted in any case.

WHEN GAME IS NOT STOPPED

25–It shall be within the discretion of the Umpire not to stop the game for the purpose of inflicting a penalty, if the stopping of the game and the infliction of the penalty would be a disadvantage to the fouled side.

RE-STARTING WHEN BALL WAS NOT OUT

26–If for any reason the game has to be stopped without the ball going out of play, it shall be re-started in the following manner.The Umpire shall stand at the spot where the ball was when the incident occurred, and facing the nearer side of the ground, but not nearer the boards or side lines than 20 yards. Both teams shall take up their own positions, each team being on its own side of an imaginary line, paralled to the goal lines and extending through the Umpire to the sides of the ground. No player may stand within five yards of the Umpire. The Umpire shall bowl the ball, underhand and hard, between the opposing ranks of players, towards the nearer side of the ground, the players remaining stationary until the ball has left his hand. If the whistle is blown for a foul at approximately the same time as the ball is hit behind the back line and the foul is over-ruled, the ball shall be thrown in as above.

TAKING PENALTIES

27–(a) **Teeing up. Making a tee is not allowed, but one player**

only may reposition the ball, provided he takes no longer than four or five seconds.

(b) Circling. Once the umpire has called "play" the striker must immediately start to take the hit. The ball must be struck or struck at on the first approach without any circling either at the beginning, during the run up or at the end.

(c) In all free hits the ball shall be in play the moment it has been either hit or hit at and missed.

DISCRETION OF UMPIRES

28–(a) Should any incident or question not provided for in the Rules of Polo, or the supplementary Rules of the Polo Association concerned, arise in a match, such incident or question shall be decided by the Umpire or Umpires. If the Umpires disagree, the Referee's decision shall be final.

(b) There are degrees of dangerous play and unfair play which give the advantage to the side fouling.The Penalty to be inflicted is left to the discretion of the Umpire or Umpires and shall only be referred to the Referee in the event of the Umpires disagreeing on the penalty.

Penalties

Note: In all free hits the ball shall be considered in play the moment it has been either hit or hit at and missed.

PENALTY GOAL

F.R. 16 17 1–(a) If, in the opinion of the Umpire, a player commits a
19 20 dangerous or deliberate foul in the vicinity of goal in order
24 to save a goal, the side fouled shall be allowed one goal.

(b) The game shall be re-started at a spot ten yards from the middle of the fouler's goal in the manner prescribed in Field Rule 26. Ends shall not be changed.

30–YARD HIT

F.R. 16 17 2–(a) A free hit at the ball from a spot 30 yards from the
19 20 goal line of the other side fouling opposite the middle of
24 the goal or, if preferred, from where the foul occurred
(the choice to rest with the Captain of the side fouled); all the side

fouling to be behind their back line until the ball is hit or hit at, but not between the goal posts, nor when the ball is brought into play may any of the side ride out from between the goal posts; none of the side fouled to be nearer the goal line or back line than the ball is, at the moment it is hit, or hit at. In the event of the Captain of the side fouled electing to take the penalty from the spot where the foul occurred none of the defending side to be within 30 yards of the ball, nor come out from between the goal posts.

(b) In carrying out Penalty 2, if the free hit would, in the opinion of the Umpire, have resulted in a goal, but is stopped by one of the side fouling coming out from between the goal posts, or crossing the back line before the ball was struck, such shot is to count as a goal to the side fouled. If the player who stopped the ball did not infringe these rules, but another member of his side did, Penalty 7 (a) shall be exacted.

40–YARD HIT

F.R. 16 17 3–(a) A free hit at the ball from a spot 40 yards from the
19 20 goal line of the side fouling opposite the middle of goal;
24 all the side fouling to be behind their back line until the ball is hit or hit at, but not between the goal posts, nor when the ball is brought into play may any of the side ride out from between the goal posts; none of the side fouled to be nearer the goal line or back line than the ball is at the moment it is hit or hit at.

(b) In carrying out Penalty 3, if the free hit would, in the opinion of the Umpire, have resulted in a goal, but is stopped by one of the side fouling coming out from between the goal posts, or crossing the back line before the ball was struck, such shot is to count as a goal to the side fouled. If the player who stopped the ball did not infringe these rules, but another member of his side did, Penalty 7 (a) shall be exacted.

60–YARD HIT (OPPOSITE GOAL)

F.R. 16 17 4–A free hit at the ball from a spot 60 yards from the goal
19 20 line of the side fouling opposite the middle of goal, none
22 of the side fouling to be within 30 yards of the ball, the side fouled being free to place themselves where they choose.

FREE HIT FROM THE SPOT

F.R. 6 15 16 17 19 20 22

5–(a) A free hit at the ball from where it was when the foul took place, but not nearer the boards or side lines than four yards. None of the side fouling to be within 30 yards of the ball, the side fouled being free to place themselves where they choose.

FREE HIT FROM THE CENTRE

(b) A free hit at the ball from the centre of the ground, none of the side fouling to be within 30 yards of the ball, the side fouled being free to place themselves where they choose.

60–YARD HIT (OPPOSITE WHERE BALL CROSSED)

F.R. 11 6–A free hit at the ball from a spot 60 yards distant from the back line, opposite where the ball crossed it, but not nearer the boards or side lines than four yards. None of the side fouling to be within 30 yards of the ball; the side fouled being free to place themselves where they choose.

ANOTHER HIT

Penalty 2, 3, 4, 5 or 6

7–(a) If the side fouling fail to carry out Penalty 2, 3, 4, 5 or 6 correctly the side fouled shall be allowed another free hit at the ball, unless a goal has been scored or awarded. If both sides fail to carry out Penalty 2 or 3 correctly, another free hit must be taken by the side fouled, irrespective of the result of the previous free hit.

HIT IN BY DEFENDERS

Penalty 2 or 3

(b) If the side fouled fail to carry out Penalty 2 or 3 correctly, the defenders shall be allowed a hit in from the middle of their own goal. None of the attacking side shall be within 30 yards of the back line until the ball is hit, or hit at; the defenders being free to place themselves where they choose.

HIT IN FROM 30-YARD LINE

F.R. 10 Penalty 7 (b)

(c) If the attacking side fail to carry out Field Rule 10 correctly the defenders shall be allowed to hit in from the 30-yard line, from the spot opposite where the first hit was made or would have been made. None of the attackers shall be within

30 yards of the ball until it is hit or hit at; the defenders being free to place themselves where they choose. For infringement of Penalty 7 (b) or any further infringement of Penalty 7 (c) by the attacking side, the defenders shall be allowed another hit from the 30–yard line.

UNNECESSARY DELAY

F.R. 10c. 27 (d) In the event of unnecessary delay by the side fouled when called on by the Umpire to take a penalty hit, the Umpire shall restart the game from the spot where the hit should have been taken in accordance with Field Rule 26.

PLAYER TO RETIRE

F.R. 24 8–Designation by the Captain of the side fouled of the player on the side fouling whose handicap is nearest above that of the disabled player, who shall retire from the game. If the handicap of the disabled player is higher than that of any of his opponents the player whose handicap is nearest below that of the disabled player may be designated. If there are two or more such players the Captain of the side fouled shall designate the one to retire. The game shall be continued with three players on each side, and if the side fouling refuses to continue the game, it shall thereby forfeit the match. This penalty does not apply to international matches.

PONY DISQUALIFIED

F.R. 3 9–(a) For infringement of Field Rule 3; the pony ordered off the ground by the Umpire and disqualified from being played again during the game or match.

Note: The case of a pony blind of an eye must be reported by the Umpire in writing to the Committee conducting the tournament who shall take all steps necessary to ensure that it shall not be played again in any tournament.

PONY ORDERED OFF

F.R. 4 (b) For infringement of Field Rule 4; pony ordered off the ground by the Umpire and disqualified from playing again until the offence has been removed.

PLAYER ORDERED OFF

F.R. 5 (c) For infringement of Field Rule 5; the player ordered off the ground by the Umpire and disqualified from playing again until he has removed the offence.

General Note: In all the above three cases play must be re-started immediately as prescribed in Field Rule 26 and the game shall continue while the player is changing his pony or removing the offence.

PLAYER EXCLUDED

10–The Umpires may exclude a player from the game, in addition to any other penalty, in the case of a deliberate foul, dangerous foul, or conduct prejudicial to the game. Alternatively, for a less serious offence, **they** may exclude a player for the rest of the chukka in progress. **In all** cases the umpires must agree or if not in agreement ask the **referee to decide**. The side to which the excluded player belonged shall continue with three players only or forfeit the match **provided the tournament committee of the club running the match agrees**.

Note 1: **If a player is sent off for the rest of a chukka, a report form must be completed by the umpires and sent to the Chief Umpire; if a player is sent off for the rest of a match, the circumstances must be reported by the umpires to the disciplinary committee of the club on whose ground the game took place. Refer to HPA Disciplinary Procedures.**

Note 2: **Continuing misconduct. A warning to a player must be given formally and in front of both captains. If a player, after being warned by the umpires for misconduct, commits similar misconduct, at the very least the umpires must penalise him; should he commit further similar misconduct, at the very least he must be sent off for the rest of the chukka. This does not preclude the umpires imposing penalty 10 – sending off – at the first offence. In all cases the umpires must both agree or if not in agreement the referee will decide.**

Rules Appendix – Examples of Field Rules

EXAMPLE I

FIELD RULE:

16 (f)	**Loss of Right of Way.**
16 (g)	**Player riding from opposite directions must take the ball on their offside.**
16 (c) (iv)	**Player riding in general direction ball is travelling entitled to Right of Way.**

The ball has been hit from X and is about to stop at XI. A is riding in the general direction in which the ball is travelling, and provided he rides to take the ball on his offside (which will necessitate his swerving to the left of the course he is shown as following) he will be entitled to the Right of Way shown. In this case B can meet the ball safely at XI, as both A and B will be taking the ball on their offside. Alternatively, a player at C could hook A's stick in safety.

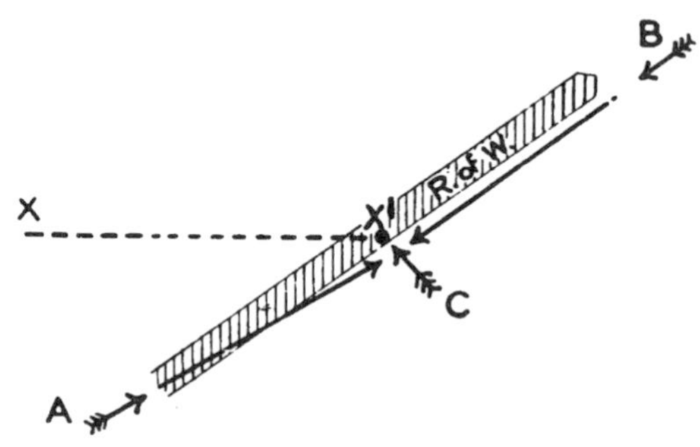

If, however, A continues on the course shown, intending to take the ball on his near side, he will endanger B or C and will therefore lose his Right of Way and so must keep clear of B or C as the case may be.

EXAMPLE II

FIELD RULE:

16 (c) (i) **Line follower entitled to Right of Way.**

16 (a) (i) **Keeping clear of Right of Way.**

A hits the ball to X, and follows its line to take it on his offside. This entitles him to the Right of Way, as shown.

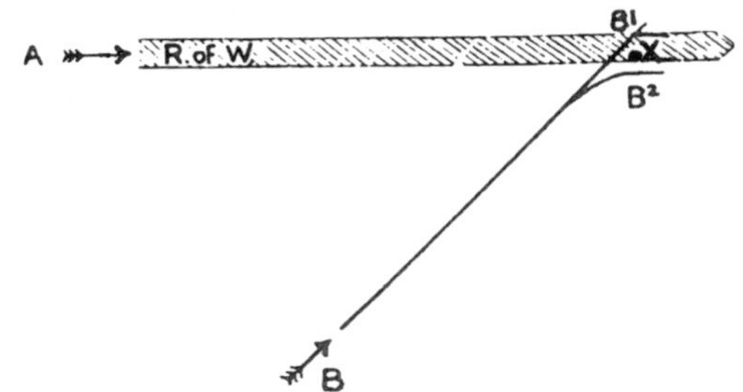

If B can unquestionably reach the ball at X, without interfering with A's stroke or causing him to check in the slightest degree to avoid the risk of a collision, then the Right of Way passes to B and he may take an offside backhander at BI.

But if there is the slightest doubt about B riding clear of A, then A's Right of Way holds good and B's only chance of hitting the ball is to swerve towards B2, keeping clear of the Right of Way, and take a near-side backhander, or afterwards, his pony in the slightest degree enters the Right of Way, he infringes Field Rule 16 (a) (i).

EXAMPLE III

FIELD RULE:

16 (e) (i) **Player meeting ball on its exact line entitled to Right of Way.**

16 (g) **Players riding from opposite directions must take the ball on their offside.**

A hits the ball in from behind to X.

B rides to meet it, C to take it on.

A collision is imminent between B and C at X.

B is entitled to the Right of Way because he is meeting the ball on its exact line to take it on his offside.

C must not cross this Right of Way.

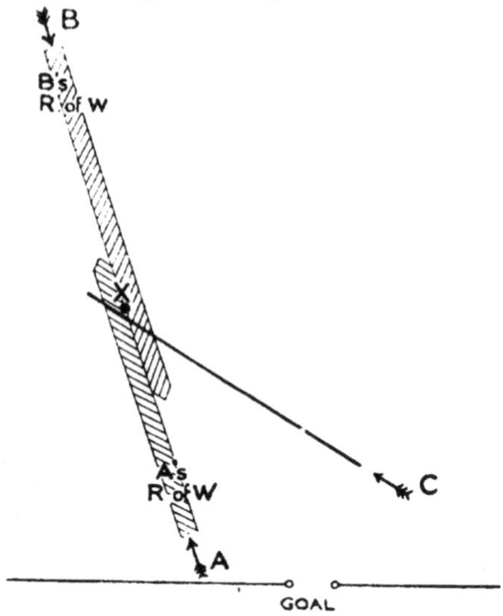

The only way for the side hitting in to take the ball on, is for A to follow its line and take an off-side shot, because A and B are each entitled to their own Rights of Way, which are clear of one another.

EXAMPLE IV

FIELD RULE:

16 (c) (iii) Two players following line of ball.

The ball has been hit from the mouth of goal to X.

The back (Red) and No.1 (Blue) are following up the line of the ball, riding each other off.

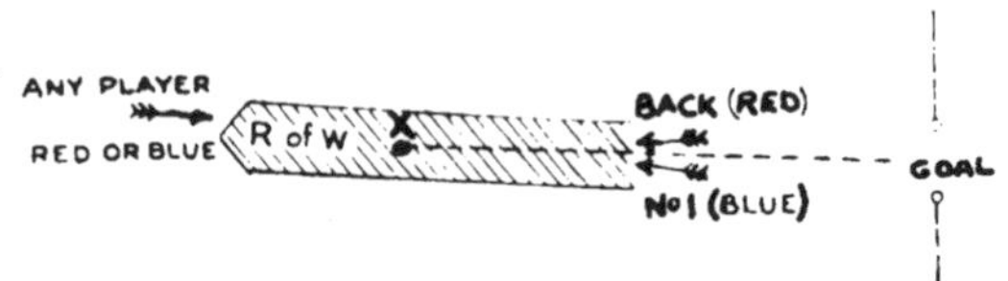

These two players share the Right of Way, as shown, and no other player, or players (Red or Blue) may cross or enter this Right of Way, even if meeting the ball on its exact line.

EXAMPLE V

FIELD RULE:

16 (c) (ii) Player following at smallest angle.

The ball has been hit to X.

Neither A nor B hit it there, but the striker is not near enough to the ball to risk a collision with either.

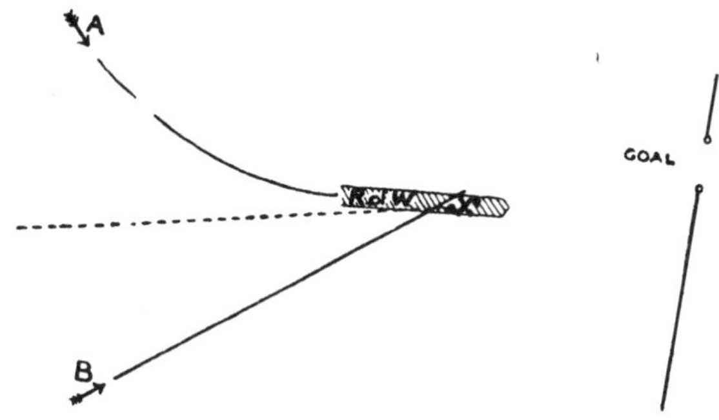

Both start to ride to the ball, with equal rights.

A collision appears probable at X.

A has the Right of Way, as shown, as he followed more closely the line on which the ball has been travelling.

EXAMPLE VI

FIELD RULE:

16 (c) (v) Right of Way not dependent on who last hit the ball.

Line follower entitled to Right of Way.

B hits the ball under his pony's neck to X, and swings round in a semi-circle to BI.

A follows the line of the ball AI.

At AI BI a collision is imminent.

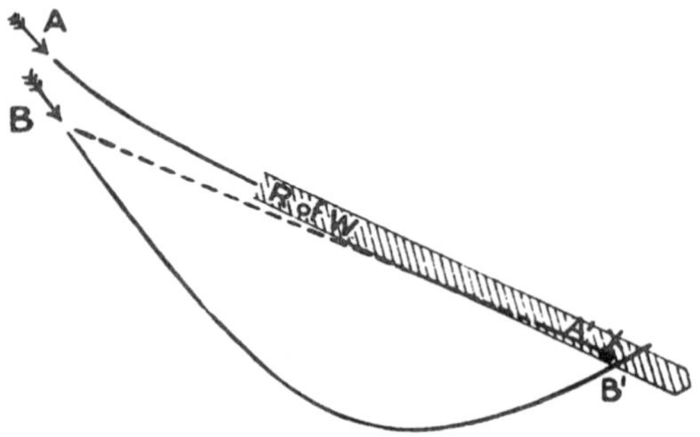

Although B hit the ball last he has failed to obtain the Right of Way because he has failed to follow the ball on its exact new line without deviation, whereas A has ridden on a line closer and more nearly parallel to the new line of the ball.

A is therefore entitled to the Right of Way.

EXAMPLE VII

FIELD RULE:

17 (d) Riding an opponent across the Right of Way.

No.2 (Red) hits the ball to X and follows its line to take it again on his offside. He is therefore entitled to the Right of Way, as shown.

The Back (Blue) rides for the ball. The No. 1 (Red) goes with him riding him off all the way.

A collision appears probable at X.

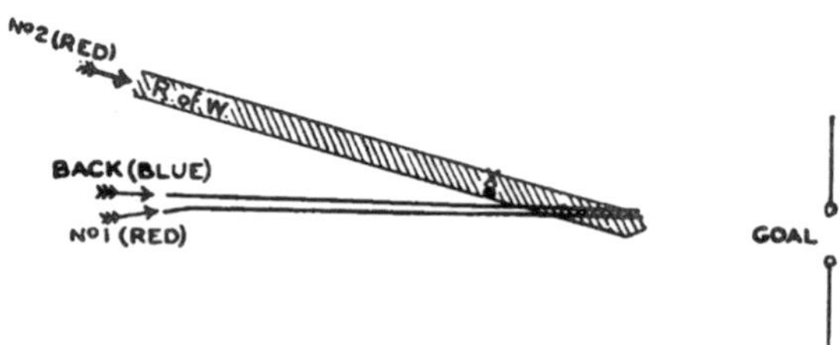

No. 1 (Red) will commit a dangerous foul if he fails to give

away and consequently:-

(a) forces the Back (Blue) across the Right of Way), thereby causing his own No.2 (Red) to check to avoid a collision, or

(b) causes the Back (Blue) to check in order to avoid being sandwiched between the two Red players.

Note: In case (a) the Umpire must observe closely whether the Back (Blue) fouls by riding across the Right of Way of his own free will or whether the No.1 (Red) fouls by forcing him across it.

Suggested Layout of a Polo Ground

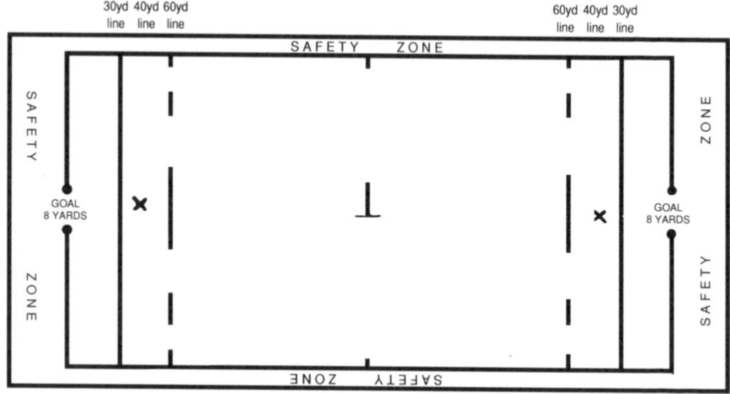

Length: 300 yards maximum, 250 yards minimum.

Breadth: 200 yards (165 yards maximum if boarded).

Safety zone: At sides about 10 yards, at ends about 30 yards.

Markings on Ground: 30-yard line straight across ground — this helps Umpires in carrying out Field Rule 10. At 40 yards a spot or a small cross exactly opposite the middle of the goals; and at 60 yards a broken line is sufficient, but there should be a line exactly four yards long from boards inwards — this enables umpires to place the ball four yards from side boards when required under Penalties 5 and 6.

Centre Line: A T in centre and marks on boards.

• The figures 30, 40 and 60 should be painted on the boards, a mark being sufficient for the centre line.

- Flags should then be used to show 30, 40 and 60 yards, but care should be taken to place then behind the side lines.

- The goals must be 8 yards apart (16 yards when playing widened goals) and at least 10 feet high. They must be capable of collapsing should there be a collision.